The Postmodern World

THE POSTMODERN WORLD

Discerning the Times and the Spirit of Our Age

MILLARD J. ERICKSON

CROSSWAY BOOKS

A DIVISION OF
GOOD NEWS PUBLISHERS
WHEATON, ILLINOIS

The Postmodern World

Copyright © 2002 by Millard J. Erickson

Published by Crossway Books
a division of Good News Publishers
1300 Crescent Street
Wheaton, Illinois 60187

Cover design: Cindy Kiple

Cover photos: PhotoDisc and Corbis

First printing 2002

Printed in the United States of America

Library of Congress Cataloging-in-Publication Data
Erickson, Millard J.
   The postmodern world : discerning the times and the spirit of our age / Millard J. Erickson.
      p.   cm.
   Includes bibliographical references and index.
   ISBN 1-58134-342-6 (trace pbk. : alk. paper)
   1. Postmodernism—Religious aspects—Christianity. I. Title.
BR115.P74 E75   2002
261.5—dc21   2001006919
                                                              CIP

15	14	13	12	11	10	09	08	07	06	05			
15	14	13	12	11	10	9	8	7	6	5	4	3	2

In memory of
John Newport, 1917–2000

Former colleague at
Southwestern Baptist Theological Seminary
Wise student of culture who loved God
with both heart and mind

CONTENTS

PREFACE

The word *postmodernism* is increasingly being mentioned, even in informal conversation. Often it is used with respect to a work of art or literature. To many persons, it is a strange word, one whose reference they do not understand. Yet the phenomenon to which that big word refers is much more familiar than most people think, for it is a label for characteristics of everyday life. Postmodernism is a particular way of looking at life, a set of ideas. It is perhaps more correctly referred to as "postmodernity," a characteristic of our culture that is gradually coming to distinguish much of human activity.

It is the purpose of this little book to enable the reader to understand and be able to recognize the phenomenon of postmodernism. Beyond that, however, because I am especially writing for evangelical Christians, I will try to help the discerning reader evaluate this phenomenon and be better prepared to deal with it. Readers who, after reading this book, wish to go on to a more technical treatment of postmodernism are encouraged to read my *Truth or Consequences: The Promise and Perils of Postmodernism* (Downers Grove, Ill.: InterVarsity, 2001).

The material contained herein has been presented a number of times to student and church groups. Among those occasions were a pastor's meeting sponsored by the Church Based Leadership Center at San Marcos, Texas, May 25, 1999; Staley Lectureships at Berry College, Mount Berry, Georgia, March 6-7, 2000; and at Toccoa Falls College, Toccoa Falls, Georgia, March 26-30, 2000; and the midweek service of Bethlehem Baptist Church, Minneapolis, Minnesota, December 3, 2000. The questions and comments I received on those occasions were of great help to me in focusing the topics for this volume. Several students in my classes on postmodernism contributed ideas to the first chapter. Maria den Boer and Bill Deckard greatly improved the manuscript with their editorial skill. I also want to thank Marvin Padgett, vice president, editorial, of Crossway Books, for encouraging me to publish this volume. It is sent forth with the hope and prayer that it may be of help to Christians in discerning and ministering to the spirit of our age.

1

POSTMODERNISM: IT'S EVERYWHERE YOU WANT TO BE

The Visa credit card company has developed a catchy and effective slogan: "Visa—it's everywhere you want to be." The ads show various situations in which a competitor's credit card is not accepted, but Visa is. In a sense, the phenomenon of postmodernism is like Visa. It's also everywhere, but the difference is that it also is in some places where you don't want to be. That it is ubiquitous is quite clear. But because it is so common and so present, we may not really be conscious of it. It is like the air we breathe. We are fully unaware of it. Perhaps when we move to a new area where there is a distinctive odor in the air (such as fumes from a paper plant), we initially notice the change in our environment. Yet we soon become accustomed to it and fail to be aware of it any longer. Likewise, because of the spreading influence of postmodernism, we may hardly notice it. It is therefore all the more important that we take special pains to identify what we are talking about.

When I say this, I am aware that I should not speak of postmodernism only in the third person, as "he, she, it, they." Because we live in a world increasingly characterized by postmodernism, and because some of us may have had our major educational experience in a culture of postmodernism, this is not some external hypothetical factor. I am reminded of what one of my students said about a chapel experience he had as an undergraduate. A noted evangelical leader had come to his school, and described and criticized the evils of postmodernism. "But," said the student, "he was like a Ku Klux Klan leader trying to enlist members at a meeting of the NAACP." Postmodernism—it's everywhere you want to be—including, perhaps, even within your own thinking.

Postmodernism by its very nature is not easy to define in simple terms. It is both a broad cultural and sociological phenomenon and an ideology, a set of ideas. Instead of beginning with a standard definition, stating certain qualities of the movement and then distinguishing it from other members of its class, we do well first to identify some instances of it, and then draw out a description. Let's look at three sketches, taken from real life.

Scene one. A young woman listens regularly to a radio station that has a talk show format. The radio host poses a different controversial issue each day, and listeners call in, offering their opinions on that topic. When asked why she listens to this type of program, the young woman responds, "These are important questions." Then, when asked why she doesn't read what experts on that subject have to say, she replies, "I like to hear different people's opinions."

Scene two. The Judiciary Committee of the United States Senate is conducting confirmation hearings on a presidential nominee for associate justice of the Supreme Court. The nominee, an African-American male, is a conservative. After extensive questioning about alleged sexual harassment, the committee turns to his educational experience. Because he attended Roman Catholic parochial schools, some more liberal members of the committee are afraid that he may believe in natural law—the idea that right and wrong are grounded in the very nature of the universe. Finally, the chairman instructs the nominee: "Right and wrong are what the United States Congress decides."

Scene three. A young man is on trial as an accessory to murder. His best friend murdered a young girl while this man stood by. When asked by the prosecutor why he did nothing to stop his friend, not even verbally, and why he did not notify anyone, the young man replies, "I didn't know the girl. I knew my friend."

Now let's go back and examine each of these sketches, noting the distinctive character of the incident, and how it exemplifies a facet of postmodernism. The first (the radio talk show) illustrates a familiar trend in our society. There was a time when the opinion of an expert, who had devoted much time to studying a given subject, was highly valued. Now, however, such expert opinion, which claims a special knowledge of the subject, is often considered irrelevant. Truth is not something objective, to be understood more and more completely. Truth is what is truth for me, and that may be different than it is for you or others. A friend of mine who is a New Testament professor says that he comes to class and offers an interpretation of a passage, on which he has spent much time and labor, building upon the years of study that he spent acquiring a doctorate in the field. When he gives his interpretation, however, a student may object, suggesting that the passage says something different to him, even though he may not have invested any time studying the passage. If the professor does not grant equal validity to the student's interpretation, he is regarded as closed-minded and authoritarian.

The second incident (the Senate hearing) is an interesting one. It also relates to truth. There are no universal values, which apply everywhere and for everyone. Nor are right and wrong different for each individual. Rather, each group sets its own standards, which are valid and normative for the group, but not beyond it. An example would be rules of the road. Is it inherently proper to drive on the right-hand side of the road, or on the left-hand side? The answer is, neither the right nor the left is intrinsically good or bad, right or wrong. In the United States, however, the laws dictate that you drive on the right, and that is what is correct. To do otherwise on a two-way road is wrong, illegal, and even immoral, under certain circumstances, should a human life be lost as a result. But what about driving in Great Britain? Here it is right to drive on the left, and wrong to drive on the right. What is the difference between these two situations? It is simply that the legislative bodies in one country have set the rules one way, while those in the other have established different laws. There is nothing inherently proper about driving on the right, so that it would be right everywhere and always.

The third case, a tragic one, illustrates a slightly different facet of postmodernism. Here, the basis for moral conviction and action is not the rights of all humans, or their value as human beings, but whether there is a communal relationship between me and the other person. Because the young man was a friend to the murderer, and there was a certain relationship between them, there was an obligation and an esteeming of value that held for his friend but not for the victim.

Now that we have considered these three instances of postmodernism, let's try a few more, four this time. Scene four is still painfully familiar to residents of the United States. The president of the United States is being tried in impeachment proceedings in the United States Senate, the House of Representatives having passed articles of impeachment. He is being tried, not for his sexual improprieties with a White House intern, but for lying to cover up his behavior. The specific charge is that he lied under oath, and thus is guilty of perjury. His attorney, however, begins his defense, not by rebutting the charges of lying under oath, but by charging that the special prosecutor was biased against the president and has been maliciously attempting to "get" him.

Scene five. Here we will take two incidents together. A large evangelical denomination in the United States announces at the time of the Jewish holy days that they are praying for the conversion of Jewish people to faith in Jesus Christ as their personal Savior. Jewish leaders and the media raise a strong protest against this practice as intolerant, and even as encouraging hate crimes against Jews. In the second incident, the pope, as the earthly head of the Roman Catholic Church, plans a trip to India. He is told, however, by officials of the Hindu religion in India that if he is to do so, he must declare that Christianity is not the only true religion or the only means of salvation. Failure to do so, they say, will promote hatred between the two groups.

15

Scene six. The Phoenix Suns National Basketball Association team has just finished a game against the Portland Trailblazers. On the team bus, the Suns' all-star power forward calls his wife on his cellular phone. During the conversation, the player passes out and collapses. He is rushed to a local hospital where, after several days, the condition is diagnosed as resulting from the player's self-medication with herbs. Armed with this knowledge, the medical personnel manage to get him out of danger and eventually restore him to health.

Scene seven. The United States Senate is debating a particular bill. Some, of a more conservative bent, who hold a "strict constructionist" view, object that this proposed bill is unconstitutional, because it is opposed to the intention that the authors of the Constitution expressed in that document. Others, who believe in a "living Constitution," contend that the authorial intent is irrelevant, that the meaning of the Constitution is what it means to us today.

Now let's revisit each of the incidents in this list and see how it exemplifies postmodernism. In scene four, the view of truth is not a question of an idea's correspondence to an objective state of affairs. Rather, the defensibility of one's actions depends upon the motivation of the person bringing the accusation. The ethical question (did he lie?) becomes subsidiary to the question of etiquette (is the prosecutor treating him politely?).

In the fifth scene, the question of religious beliefs is introduced for the first time. No coercion or threat of any kind is involved. It is simply a question of contending that if one view is correct, its contradictory cannot also be correct, and that is not allowable. In a postmodern scheme, each person's truth is truth for him or her, and to suggest that one is attempting to persuade another person of one's own truth is a rejection of that person, or a mark of disrespect. From disrespect, says this view, comes hatred. Almost every view is to be tolerated, the only exception being a view that insists upon its own absoluteness.

Now consider scene six. Traditional medicine has been strongly tied to a conventional understanding of the scientific method. Treatments were based upon an understanding of the anatomy and physiology of the human body and the chemical analysis of medications, whose effectiveness was assessed by scientific testing. Alternative medicine, however, is not bound by such restrictions. Evidence for the effectiveness of certain treatments is anecdotal, and is not accompanied by scientifically controlled assessments of the after-effects or negative results that may also have occurred. In some cases, the advocates of alternative medicine speak of traditional medicine as corrupt and narrow.

In scene seven (differing views of the U.S. Constitution) we see the redefinition of the very idea of meaning. Here, instead of meaning residing in some fixed, static content of the text, placed there intentionally by the author(s), meaning is dynamic and fluid. It depends upon the situation in which the text is being read. Indeed, the meaning of a text is a product of its content and of the meaning brought to it by the reader. As such, it cannot be locked into some past interpretation, which is then thought to be its intrinsic meaning.

These brief sketches should be sufficient to enable us to recognize the presence, indeed, virtually the omnipresence, of postmodernism. Even in places where it is most sternly resisted, evidences of its presence and influence can often be found. Let us now, however, examine in somewhat greater detail the contrast between the postmodern period and the earlier premodern and modern periods.

One of the clearest indications of our culture's outlook is television, since it has such wide exposure. Here we can also see juxtaposed the values of the current generation and the previous one by simply switching between the prime time programs of the major broadcast networks and the "retro" cable networks, such as Nickelodeon and TV Land. Some examples may help us see this.

Gunsmoke was a popular television series for approximately ten years, first as a half-hour and then as a full-hour program on Saturday nights. The program was set in nineteenth-century Dodge City, Kansas, and the hero of the program was Marshal Matt Dillon. A strong supporting cast included Doc, Kitty (the owner of the Long Branch Saloon and Matt's undeclared girlfriend), and a sequence of deputies, of which the longest-running was Festus Haggin. Crime was usually at the center of each episode's plot, although other issues, particularly family and economic, were sometimes highlighted. In spite of all the violence and even killing that took place, there was a moral quality to the program. Honesty, loyalty, and courage were all highly prized and regularly displayed. Right and wrong were objective. Good and evil were clearly contrasted. Perhaps it was true, as a University of Chicago theologian once said, that "*Gunsmoke* has a more profound doctrine of humanity than do most Christian pulpits."

In one episode, Marshal Dillon was bringing in a prisoner.

This prisoner was a former lawman with whom Matt had worked in the past. As they sat by the campfire on a night's stop during their trip to Dodge City, they reminisced about the old days and the good times they had had together. Then the prisoner said, "Matt, we've gone through a lot together. Can't you just let me escape?" "No," replied Matt, "I can't do that. It's true that we've been good friends, but that has nothing to do with it. It's my duty to bring you in." In another episode, "The Victim," a simple-minded man is in jail, charged with murder as the result of a fight over a girl. The man he killed is the son of a powerful man who controls the town and who has done much for the girl. This father has a large number of men, against whom Matt stands alone, and he wants to simply string up the accused, who he asserts does not deserve a trial. He threatens Matt, who, outnumbered, is prepared to sacrifice his life rather than agree to this short-circuiting of justice. When Matt insists that any accused deserves his day in court, the father of the dead man says, "Circumstances alter the law." "No," Matt says, "they don't." Finally, the girl testifies to what really happened, and the man is released.

A transitional program, in terms of modernism and postmodernism, is *L. A. Law.* Here we have the usual flexibility of moral standards, especially as exercised by Arnie Becker. Yet genuine moral issues are raised, generally in the context of legal cases the firm is asked to handle. Set in a court context, the issue is debated by the two opposing attorneys. Although there is a legal resolution, that does not necessarily constitute a moral resolution. There seems to be an underlying assumption that there is a moral right and a moral wrong, and yet the determination

19

or the interpretation of that right or wrong is based on a given community's standards, termed "laws." It is not, however, beyond the program's reach to challenge some of those standards, to question whether a given law is really moral in light of some higher basis for morality, which is not really specified.

Another mediating program is *Frasier*. Here conventional sexual morality is not maintained, especially by Roz and Bulldog but also by Frasier. There is, however, an underlying moral tone, especially displayed by Frasier. He often agonizes over decisions and actions, going to great lengths to rectify them. His father, Martin, a retired police officer, frequently encourages Frasier to lighten up on some of these concerns, trying to keep peace and smooth social functioning. The underlying basis for these values is not discussed, although one is left to surmise that the two psychiatrists, Frasier and his brother Niles, see something inviolable about human nature and human rights.

Contrast these programs with *Seinfeld*, perhaps the paradigmatic postmodern program of the 1990s. Not only do the characters not display moral fiber, they do not even think in terms of moral issues. Their concerns are, from a moral standpoint, trivial. They are interested in pleasure, amusement, curiosity. Such issues as sexual morality do not really arise in connection with sex outside marriage. Sex becomes a matter of pleasure, even diversion. Extremely seldom, if ever, are questions of the moral rightness or wrongness of an action considered. Rather, personal convenience becomes a major factor. Consider, for example, the episode entitled "The Rye." Jerry, wanting a particular kind of bread, finds that an elderly lady has bought the last loaf and refuses to part with it. He then mugs her to get that loaf. The moral issue of stealing does not seem to be a factor. Similarly, deceit is frequently used (especially by George) when it serves the needed purpose.

One interesting feature of the series is the way what is generally termed essentialism (which we will explore in chapter 2) is rejected. This extends even to the rejection of the fixed personality. Kramer in particular is always remaking himself and his reality using the latest gadget or contrivance. In one episode he vows to get rid of all of the furniture in his apartment, replacing it with levels of pillows. In another, he decides never to leave the bathroom. He purchases a waterproof television set, and installs a disposal in the drain so that he can cook in the bathroom. At other times, the characters recreate to such an extent that they actually become another character entirely. Kramer, finding an old set for a television program, takes on the persona of Merv Griffin and conducts a talk show in his living room. J. Peterman, Elaine's boss, likes to create wild stories about his exploits. He buys Kramer's biographical information, which is itself a fiction, in order to publish it as his own. George particularly pretends to be someone or something other than he is. He masquerades as an executive in the import/export business, and also pretends to be a handicapped person. The morality of such behavior is not really an issue in the program, only the problematic consequences of being discovered.

Another interesting feature of the *Seinfeld* show is the relationship of reality to art. Programs begin and end with Jerry doing his standup comedy routine; the material that intervenes illustrates what he is talking about. Yet here, Jerry the comedian is part of the drama that he is talking about. In other words, we are introduced to two levels of reality with Jerry, the comedian and the actor. In the episode "The Pilot," George and Jerry work on a new show for NBC. It resembles the show *Seinfeld*, with characters representing George, Elaine, and Kramer. When asked by network executives what the show is about, George responds, "Nothing! It's a show about nothing!" which also reveals its resemblance to the *Seinfeld* show. This is a show fictionalizing the fiction of the show—a show within a show, as it were.

This is a technique sometimes used in film as well. For example, *The French Lieutenant's Woman* is the story of the making of a movie that involves a romance between the two characters in the plot, but also a romance between the actor and actress who are playing those two characters. Here is reality on two levels, and yet, both levels are still within the film, a film about a film. We are still on the outside, looking into a room, and through the window looking out on the reality being observed by the people in the room. This same feature can be seen in newscasts. In the past, the newspersons were seen on the set. They still are throughout the program, but now, at the end of the newscast, the director switches to a camera farther from the set than the others, and one sees not only the set, but the cameras, camera persons, and so on. Similarly, note the practice of appending at the end of a program the gaffs that took place in earlier recordings, a practice especially common on *Home Improvement*. While the interpretation of these practices is debated, it appears that one effect is to blur the line between reality and construct, or to suggest that one cannot be sure what reality actually is. What is being done, of course, in the case of newscasts, is to undermine confidence in the reality of the report of the news, whether the producers realize it or not.

Sometimes words or symbols are seen as referring not to something outside the interplay of such symbols, but as referring only to other symbols. This appears in an interesting episode of *Seinfeld*. Kramer has written a coffee-table book about coffee tables, and appears on *Regis and Kathie Lee Live* to discuss it. He then reveals that the book has folding legs, so that the coffee-table book about coffee tables can itself become a coffee table.

Seinfeld, then, is a program about nothing. Yet actually, by not being about any subject, having no moral, it is itself telling a story about the world. There is no objective right and wrong, only what forwards one's own cause, or helps or hurts one's own community. The truth is also blurred, not only by the techniques we have described but also by the way the truth is manipulated. George, for example, convinces his parents to move to Florida, which he wants, by persuading them that the senior Seinfelds, their rivals of sorts, don't want them to move there. Even when there is a concern to discover the truth, the truth sought is all part of the value system of the characters, as when Jerry goes to great lengths to determine whether his girlfriend's figure is genuine or fake. Convictions are means of utility, particularly for George. In "The Conversion," he considers converting to the Latvian Orthodox Church, because a girl he is interested in will not date anyone from a different background. On another occasion, he cheats on an IQ test by having Elaine take it for him, so he can get into Mensa and impress a girl. Interestingly, although the characters' moral indifference to the plight of a mugged man in the final episode of *Seinfeld* leads to their arrest and imprisonment, that conviction takes place in a small rural town, not in their own community (although witnesses from New York are called). It is as if such moral convictions are defined by a different community, one that is a throwback to another era.

It is interesting to note some other subtle indications of postmodernism's presence. For example, for many years there was what I call the "white jacket" ad. This ad involved an expert, a scientist, who testified regarding the effectiveness of a product. Frequently, the wearer of the white jacket was a medical doctor, recommending a particular medical product. The subliminal message was that science, with all of its supposed objectivity and certainty, certified the value of this product. This type of appeal has now changed, however. Such white jacket depictions, while still to be found, are generally less frequent, and when present, are often more indirect and even incidental. For example, in one ad a man tells of the digestive discomfort he experienced while on a plane. His seatmate recommends that he try a particular antacid, which he does and gets relief from his distress. According to his account, he says to the other man, "Maybe I should see a doctor," to which the other replies, "You just did!" The man then says into the camera, "Thanks, Doc, wherever you are out there."

Note, however, several significant features of the ad. For one thing, the doctor never appears on the screen. He is simply a character in the narrative that the man recounts, and even if he had been there, he would not have been wearing the white coat. He was a doctor, but he was not in his official capacity, in which patients make office visits. This was just a casual meeting with a stranger who turned out to be a doctor, and presumably no fee was charged or paid. And the final testimony to the value of the medication is not experimental studies of its effectiveness, but rather, the personal experience of the man who took it and got some relief.

Sometimes the shift is even more obvious. In another ad, a woman tells of the pain relief she has received by taking a particular product. Then she says, "How do I know it works? Oh, they have research and reports, but I don't care about all that. I know what it did for me." Here is the rejection, or at least the discounting, of the modern paradigm's reliance on the efficacy of natural science. What really counts is personal experience. The implication, of course, is that what worked for her will also work for the listener, but since that is not made explicit, it does not require demonstration or argument.

Many other popular expressions of postmodernism can be seen. One characteristic of the modern period was organization, structure, and orderliness. The relative places of each member of an organization or society were clearly spelled out and usually identified by some obvious means. This has taken various forms, from the location of an office in a building, to the size of the desk, to the person's title. Often a person's place within society was apparent from what he or she wore, so that "blue collar" and "white collar" distinguished manual laborers from clerical and professional workers. Even the way a person was addressed was significant. "Doctor," or "the Reverend," or "the Honorable," are examples of this. Whether the first name or the last name of the person was used indicated relative rank, assuming that there was some acquaintance between the two. The most highly structured version of this is of course the military. On the one occasion that I visited the Pentagon, I was struck by how you could tell at a glance not only the person's last name but also his or her rank. Even persons lower in rank were identified by last name and rank, rather than by first name.

While there are still examples of the modern period and structure today, evidences of change are all around us. Casual is in as far as dress is concerned. It is now difficult to distinguish the president of a firm from a lowly clerk in the organization. This is particularly true in parts of the country such as California, and in certain fields such as technology, perhaps in part because these fields are heavily populated by younger people. The only people who wear identifying uniforms today are usually those who serve the public in some direct way, such as waitresses, hotel employees, or mechanics. Titles also are less frequently used, and first names are used by persons who have never met. I recall being particularly struck by this when I was the executive vice president and dean of a seminary. I received a telephone call from a young student recruiter at the college associated with our seminary. Although we had never met, she immediately addressed me by my first name. I thought to myself, "This is a new era. I never would have called the dean of the seminary I attended, 'Ed,' particularly on my first contact with him."

The phenomenon appears in other contexts as well. "Grade inflation" is an example. There was a time when student grades were somewhat normally distributed over the spectrum of letter categories. An A was a truly distinctive grade, representing real achievement, and even a B was cause for a sense of satisfaction. C's were respectable indications of satisfactory work. Only

D's and F's carried any real stigma. Now, however, the A and B brackets are so crowded that one cannot from the letter grade discern truly outstanding or exceptional work from that which is merely good. To receive a C is humiliating for most college students. D's are very scarce, and in many institutions, F's, once the sign of failure, have become extinct, replaced by the more neutral "no credit." In one institution where I taught, it was possible to obtain a Ph.D. degree, which looked on paper like any other Ph.D., with a dissertation that had been graded "Unsatisfactory, but not failing." Whereas a 3.0 or B average once qualified a student for honors such as cum laude, the bar has had to be raised much higher. The effect is a leveling of the academic population. The opinions of truly excellent students and those who are little above average are treated equally. The same phenomenon can be observed with respect to academic titles. The term *chancellor* was once reserved for the head of a multicampus system, but now may be a glorified title for "president emeritus." Similarly, a provost was once the chief academic officer of a multischool university, with the deans of these several schools reporting to him. Now provost is in some cases a glorified name for the dean of a single-school institution. What were once termed departments or divisions are now schools or centers, each with its own "dean."

All of this is part of the minimization of knowledge as the solution to human problems. In the modern period, the person who had studied, achieved excellence in mastery of his or her field, and had applied intensive effort to the solution of the problem at hand was believed to be a more reliable source of insight than someone who merely offered an opinion on the subject. Today, opinions count more.

One phenomenon that has not received a great deal of attention is the status of laws in a postmodern age. For the most part, there is a lesser concern for the fulfillment of or abiding by laws than in earlier times. To follow laws, especially in an undeviating manner, is thought to be "legalism," which is deemed a very bad thing. Freedom to deviate from such regulations is a positive virtue. Often, when pressed for a rationale for such action, the reply given is, "We are more interested in people than in rules." On the surface of it, at least, this appears to be the concern for community that is such a hallmark of postmodernism. Yet something of a paradox is involved in this sort of behavior. For laws are usually understood as having been enacted for the good of the community as a whole. They are the means by which those members of the community who are weaker or less able to defend their rights are protected from the stronger. Those whom the community has selected to represent it have put those laws in place.

There is another paradox here, however. In Lawrence Kohlberg's levels of moral development, acting on the basis of obedience to laws is one of the lower levels. To challenge laws is frequently represented as being a movement from the "conventional" to the "postconventional," in which one uses certain moral principles to evaluate and choose to follow or disregard laws. It should be noted, however, that unwillingness to follow laws may also issue from a lower level, a "preconventional" level. One may simply want to fulfill personal desires, in the face of which such laws are an obstruction. Interestingly, this is fre-

28

quently the case. I have observed professors who dislike administrators "going by the book" when it works to their personal disadvantage, but who insist upon procedures when it is to their benefit. What we have here is a type of community, but a community that insists upon its own welfare at the expense of the larger community. As such, it is only a collective individualism.

I recall serving on the Educational Policies Committee of a college that required two years of Reserve Officer Training Corps (ROTC) for all male students. Strong protest against this requirement was lodged on the basis of conviction regarding the morality of the Vietnam War, which was still going on at the time. The committee met every afternoon for the final two weeks of the school year, trying to find a solution to the impasse. Finally, one member of the committee, with more experience and insight into those undergraduates than I had, proposed a compromise. ROTC would still be required, but only for one year. To my surprise, this proposal met with quick and unreserved acceptance by the student community. The principled convictions about the immorality of the war and of requiring students to take ROTC quickly faded in light of the realization that the requirement would no longer apply to any of the students then on campus (who would have already served their one year!). This reaction came from a student generation whose slogan was, "Don't trust anyone *over* thirty!" Recent studies on cheating practices indicate that the exact opposite was true, even then.

Logical consistency is not a distinctive of the postmodern age, either in thought or in practice, and sometimes *between* thought and practice. In some ways, John F. Kennedy was the first postmodern president. Apart from the question of the extra-marital affairs in which he engaged, even in the White House, there was the split between personal convictions and public policy. This first showed up when the issue of his Roman Catholicism surfaced during the presidential election campaign. Kennedy insisted that his personal religious practice and beliefs would not have any effect upon his conduct in the presidency. Similarly, there was a contradiction between his public policy and personal practice. Kennedy's political sentiments were strongly oriented toward programs that would help the poor, no doubt a sincere political conviction. Yet the entire Kennedy clan maintained a lavish lifestyle at their compound on Cape Cod, and it is alleged that during each year that he occupied the White House, his wife Jacquelyn spent in excess of $300,000 on her personal wardrobe. This split between public policy and personal practice is what I have come to refer to as "The Kennedy Syndrome."

Often these apparent lapses in practice appear in strange places. I recall eating with a group in a restaurant with a young woman who complained to the waitress, from an animal rights perspective, about the presence of a certain item on the menu. The waitress, at the end of the meal, pointed out to the young woman that she was wearing a fur coat.

Even attire does not necessarily demonstrate consistency. I grew up in a time in which attire was coordinated. If you wore a business suit, you did not wear sports shoes with it, and if you were clad in jeans, you did not combine them with a dress shirt and tie. Yet I recall a small and informal wedding at which the groom had bought a very nice suit for the occasion. His best man was his brother, and their mother was very disturbed that although he was dressed in a nice sport coat, dress shirt, and tie, he was wearing blue denim jeans. Her efforts to convince him to change to more appropriate slacks were of no avail.

It may, of course, be objected that these considerations are merely anecdotal. I would point out, however, that the aim here is to illustrate, not prove, the extensiveness of postmodernism's influence. The reader is encouraged to ask himself or herself whether these incidents are completely unique and atypical.

A further characteristic of the postmodern age is a reduced sense of commitment. There was a time when people possessed brand loyalty. Whether it was economically prudent or not, some persons simply were Chevrolet people, while others always drove a Ford. Sometimes this brand loyalty carried over to subsequent generations in the family. Brand loyalty was also manifested in commitment to a religious denomination, so a Presbyterian would look for a Presbyterian church when moving to a new community, as a Methodist would seek out a Methodist church to attend. This was a lifelong commitment, and would not be deviated from without a very strong and compelling reason for doing so.

The same thing was true in marriages. It was expected that love would lead to the institution of marriage, with the legal and other commitments that involved. The marriage vows included expressions about "from this day forward . . . till death do us part," and those vows were taken seriously. It was expected that the union would be permanent, and that it would be exclusive on the part of both parties. That has changed, however. Many persons, attracted to each other, simply take up housekeeping together, without the legal bonds of matrimony. Severing such arrangements is relatively less complicated legally, although "palimony" suits have been brought against former (unmarried) lovers. Marriages also are not necessarily expected to be permanent. If the marriage proves disappointing, it can be dissolved and another one entered into.

Take vocational commitments. At one time, Christian missions was considered a lifetime calling. Increasingly, however, persons enter missions service with the idea that if it does not work out, or proves unsatisfying, they can move to a different life activity. Beyond that, short-term missions, sometimes as short as one or two weeks, are becoming increasingly popular. In voluntary organizations, long-term commitments are even more difficult to obtain. The idea of a pledge or other commitment to an ongoing program of financial giving has no appeal to many present-day persons, as is true of the idea of committing oneself to being present and active week after week as a volunteer.

One other indication of postmodernism can be seen in music. Some contemporary music, both secular and sacred, seems to deemphasize the intellectual or cognitive dimension. Volume is so loud as almost to overwhelm the individual's consciousness, and sometimes includes an actual physical vibration. The content is often minimal, is of the most concrete or basic form, and often is repeated numerous times, in some cases in almost mantra-like fashion. This is sometimes accompanied by a shift of key. The effect is to bypass the reflective or critical dimension of experience. One simply feels, rather than thinks about, what is happening.

Let us examine one more case. A seminary faculty is deliberating over a case of student discipline. One student has, over a period of time, consistently asked to substitute additional written papers for examinations, contending that he does much better writing papers than taking examinations. Gradually, some of the faculty have become suspicious that the work he is submitting may not be his own, especially when he turns in unusually good work. The matter comes to a final focus, however, when the student submits a paper containing considerable German quotations, although subsequent investigation reveals that he has a very limited knowledge of the German language.

A meeting is arranged involving the student, two of his professors, and the seminary dean. Under questioning, the student admits that the papers he has submitted are not his own work. Because of his heavy time commitment to outside ministry, he has not had time to do his academic work, and has resorted to using the work of others.

The seminary faculty deliberates as to what disciplinary action should be taken. Because the student estimates that about six courses involved this illegitimate work, one segment of the faculty believes that he should be suspended for one quarter, and required to prepare his own papers in place of the six that were illegitimate. Another segment of the faculty, however, contends that to do so would be to assess a punishment or a punitive treatment. They believe that Christian forgiveness means that he should be allowed to continue without any sort of punishment. One member of this group even questions the orthodoxy of the other group's belief in the atonement. The first group retorts that they are not assessing a penalty; the student is simply being asked to do what other students in the seminary have done. A penalty would be the addition of other requirements beyond the standard ones. In the end, a compromise is reached. The student is required to submit new papers, which are his own work, in three of the six courses.

How does this illustrate postmodernism? First, note that to the student, cheating was not a big issue, at least not initially. Because he was engaged in a ministry that was benefiting people, and because persons are more important than are rules, the end justified the means. When the faculty must decide on an appropriate disposition of the student's case, the issue is made an emotional rather than a rational one. The question of whether the standards for passing a course should be maintained is subjugated to emotional issues of sentimental concern for the student. And the decision to compromise, to find something where no one really wins or loses, is a reflection of the non-fixity of moral values and of the elevation of the community over any externally based moral standards.

After this brief survey of popular American culture, it should be apparent that postmodernism is indeed everywhere. But who are the thinkers that are developing the theoretical basis of this movement? It is to them and their ideas that we turn in the following chapter.

2

POSTMODERNISM
IN THE UNIVERSITY

We have noted the various manifestations of postmodernism in popular culture. This is the type of postmodernism displayed by people who may never have even heard the word. This is simply the way they think, feel, and act. Corresponding to this, however, is the sort of postmodernism that we meet in formal scholarly circles, the more self-conscious system of thinking worked out by intellectuals. Francis Schaeffer suggests that the progression of what he calls the "line of despair" is from philosophy to art to music to the general culture and, finally, to theology.[1] He observes that when Georg Hegel first propounded his idea of the dialectic, it must have seemed very abstruse and far removed from the practical experience of the ordinary person. Hegel's idea was that history moves in a regular pattern. Whether a belief, a political force, or a movement, there is an initial element, called the thesis, followed by its opposite, or antithesis, and these then are merged, in a synthesis. Few people ever heard of this theory, or understood it if they did. Karl Marx, however, took Hegel's theory and gave it a different form, in which it is the pattern of economics, moving toward a society in which there are neither rich nor poor. In this form, Hegel's theory eventually had a profound effect on millions of people, especially the large numbers who lived under communism. There is such a thing as a trickle-down effect in economics, and it also is true in the areas of belief and life. Whether Schaeffer's analysis of the sequence of this development is correct, his general point surely is. Many intellectual theories never take hold upon large numbers of intellectuals, but those that do eventually have an impact on popular culture. Those lower in the process do not know why they think and feel as they do, what it is that is affecting them, but they are affected nonetheless. It is therefore important that we look more closely at the thought of the theoreticians of postmodernism. Just as intermarriage involving different groups modifies descendants genetically, so these ideas get intermingled with others and the end result on the popular level is somewhat different from the pure sources. Thus, it is helpful to see just what the original sources were saying.

The Rejection of Real Essences

The first major point in our look at the roots of postmodernism is the rejection of essentialism, which takes several forms in different postmodern thinkers. In general, essentialism is the idea that things have real qualities, independent of our knowing them. Essentialism rejects the familiar statement that "Beauty is in the eye of the beholder," at least taken in a literal or extreme sense. An essentialist holds that the quality of beauty is something present in the object, although different people observing it may see it and appreciate it differently. Similarly, language has meaning, independent of our hearing, reading, or understanding it. A well-known conundrum asks, "If a tree falls in the wilderness and there is no one there to hear it, is there any sound?" The answer of the essentialist would be yes. Meaning or reality may be thought of as having any one of a number of possible bases. One variety, widely held in the earlier period known as the premodern, and prior to about the seventeenth century, was that meaning or truth is based on something outside our world. In the religious version, this is God, whose mind is the source and the locus of truth. In a more philosophical version, this was thought of as a great network of rationality, characterizing the whole of reality. The Greek philosopher Plato, for example, believed in the Ideas, which were pure essences or formulas for qualities found in the world. For instance, all beautiful things are beautiful because they participate in the Idea of Beauty. There would be Beauty whether there were any beautiful things or not.

In the later period, known as the modern period, the basis of this meaning or truth changed. Instead of being based on something outside the physical world, it was thought of as being within the system of nature. It was thought of as real characteristics of nature, or laws found in the observable world.

This idea of real essences of things has been challenged by a number of postmodern thinkers, however. One of the most emphatic of these is Jacques Derrida. Derrida, a Frenchman born in Algeria, is essentially a philosopher, who has studied at length the thought of philosophers such as Hegel, the existentialist Heidegger, and the phenomenologist Husserl, as well as ancient philosophers such as Plato. He strongly objects to what he calls "logocentrism," the idea that the meaning of things centers on a self-existent reason in the universe, whether that is thought of as deriving from the mind of God or from some patterns of reality found within the world.[2]

This essentialism or logocentrism views the world as being like a statue, which is structured and formed when we come to it. By contrast, reality in Derrida's view is more like Play-Doh, formless, which the person structures by his or her own activity. What it is, is not already there, but is created by the person, according to his or her own intentions.

One way that Derrida expresses this idea is with his concept of writing. Customarily, going all the way back to the Greeks, speech had been regarded as superior to writing. This was because it was thought to be less easily misunderstood. In speech, both the parties are present to each other (at least before the days of telephones, radios, and recorders), and the object of their conversation is often present as well. Thus, it was possible to ask about statements that were unclear, and to gain elaboration and explication.

Derrida, however, considers writing preferable to speaking. The very disadvantages that some have attributed to writing he considers to be values. For in writing, the reader can build up the meaning of words. This is done by the process of *differance*. Derrida uses this French term to speak of both differing and deferring.[3] He notes the way words are usually defined. Ordinarily a term is placed in a class, and then differentiated from other members of that class. Indeed, the word *define* means to make finite, or to limit. For example, a cow may be initially classified as a mammal, and then defined further by showing how it differs from other members of the mammal class. This is what Derrida does with words, spinning out the various meanings and eliminating some of the possibilities. In so doing, he is also engaged in deferring, as one possible definition is supplanted by another. In Derrida's method, however, the process of deferring and of defining never ends. It never comes to a point of finality in which one has *the truth.* If the meaning were an independent, objective essence, the process of definition would approximate that essence ever more closely. However, since meaning according to Derrida is not an objective essence, no such closure is possible.

An illustration here may help. In the comic strip "Peanuts," Charlie Brown and his friends are lying on the grass looking at the clouds that drift by overhead. One of his friends sees in one cloud a famous painting. Charlie Brown, however, is somewhat embarrassed because he was going to suggest that it was only a horsey and a sheep. Each person finds something different, and no one can say that his or her label is the final and correct one. This is an ongoing and unending process, in part because the cloud continues to change and re-form. In a very real sense, the cloud has no shape or pattern. There are only elements, which can be interpreted in various ways by different people.

This same conception comes through in Derrida's discussion of the judge and justice. In popular opinion, what is done is that the judge makes a decision in a given case by ascertaining the "right" answer. He looks for statutes that apply and for cases establishing precedence, and then applies these appropriate criteria to the case in question to determine the just ruling. The conception here is that justice already exists, and the role of the judge is simply to discover and announce that justice. From Derrida's perspective, however, justice is not a preexisting quality. The judge brings justice, in this particular case, into existence by his own decision. He does not discover justice; he produces it. He cannot simply follow some pre-set rules.

There is an old story about three umpires who were discussing the calling of balls and strikes. One announced confidently, "I call them as they are." The second said, "I call them as I see them." The final umpire said, "They ain't neither balls nor strikes until I call them." For purposes of our discussion here, that third umpire would represent Derrida's position. Justice does not exist until the judge makes a ruling, not merely discovering justice but creating it.

This same antipathy to the idea of independently existing truth and values can also be found in the work of the late Michel Foucault, another French philosopher. In my college sophomore introductory psychology course, the professor said, "The only difference between the people in mental institutions and those of us outside of them is that there are more of us. If there were more of them, they would put us inside." I thought at the time that he was joking, which of course he was. I never imagined that someday someone would formulate a whole theory based on this conception, but then, to my amazement, I discovered that Foucault had.

Foucault engages in what he terms "genealogy," tracing the history of institutions. He observes that during the Middle Ages, there were numerous leprosariums, designed to isolate those with leprosy from others. Gradually, however, with progress in medicine, the number of cases of leprosy declined sharply. Now many large buildings stood empty. Governments, however, did not allow this wasteful condition to continue. They began placing the poor, the unemployed, the ill, the mentally ill, and criminals into these institutions. Those in positions of power decided who should be placed in them. Power was the means of determining normality, not by discovering it but by decreeing it.

In these situations, the aim was control of the powerless by the powerful. This was done in several ways. One major instrument of control was through observation. The prisoners' lives were subject to constant scrutiny. Philosopher Jeremy Bentham designed a layout called the panopticon. This was a semicircular design, with the guard station in the center and the cells around the outside edge, each with a door on the inside and a window on the outside. From the central position the guard could look into each cell without moving from his station. With one sweep of his eyes he could simultaneously observe every prisoner. The life routine of the prisoners was also closely regulated.

This same pattern is repeated in other institutions, such as hospitals, schools, and the military. In each of these cases, those possessing power decide what those under their control are to do. Foucault, however, makes one additional, rather surprising declaration. We are accustomed to hearing that knowledge makes power. The more learning one acquires and the more skills one possesses, the more power he or she will have. Foucault, however, maintains that the relationship between power and knowledge is not monodirectional. Not only is it true that knowledge produces power, but power also produces knowledge. What, however, does he mean by such a statement? Foucault is claiming that just as those who have the power to

41

do so determine what is normal and abnormal, and what is legal and illegal, so also those with the necessary power determine what the truth is. How is this done? Again, it is by the exercise of control. In an educational institution, the teacher or the professor has decided what the "right" views on various subjects are. Consequently, the teacher decides what viewpoints the student hears on each subject. Similarly, those in authority determine the curriculum, so that what and how the student learns is controlled. Foucault says, for example, that in French schools the curriculum is historically based, so that students do not really get exposure to contemporary problems in a field.[4]

Foucault's contention is that truth is not simply something that exists independently of the knower, so that whoever discovers it is in possession of the truth. Rather, what one knows and believes to be true is a product of one's historical and cultural situation. This can be observed in a number of ways. For example, all of my formal education took place in the Midwest. I had never been a student in an institution of higher education farther south than 59th Street on the south side of Chicago. I had received a particular interpretation of what northerners called "the Civil War." When I began teaching in the South, I discovered that my students had received a somewhat different interpretation of the same conflict, which they termed "the War Between the States," or in some cases referred to as "the War of Northern Aggression." Similarly, my doctoral mentor, a Canadian, found that his son, studying history in the public schools of Evanston, Illinois, was taught a somewhat different perspective on the American Revolution than he had been exposed to in Canadian schools. This is precisely Foucault's point. What is the truth? That all depends upon who has decided what is to be learned or what the truth is.

American philosopher Richard Rorty makes a similar point, but from a different perspective. He objects to what he terms the "mirror theory" of reality, the concept that our ideas simply reflect the way reality is. The basis of that theory is that reality exists independently of our knowing it. We want to grasp and understand that reality, with our ideas reproducing the external world as closely as possible. This approach leads to what he terms Philosophy. Such an endeavor seeks to determine "what is true?" "what is good?" and similar questions. In this search for the objective realities of Truth and Virtue, one theory has replaced another in succession.

Because this approach has not proven fruitful, in Rorty's judgment, it ought to be abandoned. This response of abandonment, however, should not be thought of as a response from a superior position, but simply as a change of subject. The different kind of philosophy he intends to practice is pragmatism, which he refers to as philosophy with a small *p*. Instead of looking for a better answer to questions such as what is true and what is good, this type of philosophy simply wishes to abandon the pursuit of them. This is a direct consequence of the pragmatists' view of truth. They do not hold that truth is the correct correspondence to some state of affairs. Consequently, it is no longer necessary to investigate that state of affairs. Instead of asking such a question, the pragmatist simply asks, "Does it work?" "What would be the consequences of holding such a view?"[5]

The usual procedure when we ask a "what?" question, such

as "what is truth?" or "what is good?" is to follow it with a "why?" question, such as "why should I believe this?" or "why should I act in this way?" We may put it in the form of a "how?" question, asking "How do I know this is true?" or "How do I know this is good?" but the effect is the same either way. Rorty is proposing a radically different approach. He intends to concentrate on the "what" question. Suppose, he says, we have determined the circumstances under which a given view came to be held—the when, where, and how of such a belief. Is there then, he asks, anything else to determine? He observes that representatives of both the philosophical and the pragmatic view of truth and of ethics hold that persons have rights worth dying for. Traditionally, however, Philosophy says, in effect, "So people have come to believe this. But should they?" By this, the philosopher generally means, "Is this belief true?" This is a question of the relationship of such beliefs to Reality. What Rorty proposes instead is simply an explanation in terms of what has brought it about that the person believes this particular view. He terms this a behavioristic approach to philosophy, asking for the cause of someone's believing something, rather than the reasons for which it should be believed.

Rorty recognizes the quality of significant discoveries, such as DNA, the Big Bang theory, and so on. We should be content, however, with the fact that they have come into belief because of certain causal factors, but not press the further question, "But are they true?" He says of Aristotle's use of *ousia*, Paul's use of *agape*, and Newton's use of the concept of *gravitas*: "for all we know, or should care [these ideas] were the results of cosmic rays scrambling the fine structure of some crucial neurons in their respective brains. Or, more plausibly, they were the result of some odd episodes in infancy — some obsessional kinks left in these brains by idiosyncratic traumata. It hardly matters how the trick was done. The results were marvelous. There had never been such things before."[6]

The Rejection of Universal Explanations

Intellectual postmodernism is further distinguished by a profound aversion to all-inclusive explanations, or "metanarratives," as they have come to be known. From earliest times, humans have attempted to propound some such account of the "big picture," to identify the fundamental character of reality. The early Greek philosophers proposed various theories of this type. One speculated that everything was water, another that everything was air. One even conjectured that everything was composed of atoms of matter. In more modern times, some, who came to be known as idealists, postulated that reality was of the nature of mind, while others held that the material was the key to understanding the whole. There were, of course, numerous religious metanarratives. Christians believe that there is a great, unlimited God, who has created everything, is in control of all that happens, and is moving history toward his intended goals. One of Christianity's major competitors until its recent dissolution was communism, or, as known by its philosophical name, dialectical materialism. This worldview held that material forces are driving history, that what lies behind everything is the dialectical pattern contained within matter. The dialectic moves through a series of events and institutions, to each of which there arises a contradiction or antithesis, and then a synthesis of these

45

results. Another of Christianity's competitors, Freudian psycho-analysis, sees human behavior as driven by sexual forces, and much of what results comes from the repression of such desires.

Despite this long history of comprehensive schemes of explanation, postmodernism adamantly rejects such schemes. It does so for a variety of reasons. In Derrida, there is a sense that any such all-enveloping view is necessarily achieved by sup-pressing contradictory elements. He believes that every set of beliefs contains contradictory factors. So, for example, he dis-tinguishes between Plato's writings and Platonism. Platonism is the system that philosophers have made out of the thoughts contained within Plato's writings. In order to achieve such a system, however, it is necessary to smooth over certain ele-ments that do not fit with it. Derrida's aim is to "deconstruct" this and any other philosophy by identifying and highlighting these negative factors. Note that the term is not *construction* or *destruction*, but *deconstruction*. It is a disassembling of that which has been constructed.

If we think of the metanarrative as being like a large build-ing, composed of many pieces, then the task of deconstruction would be to break up the monolith. Deconstruction does this by calling attention to the extraneous factors. If these are removed, then that which purports to rest upon them would collapse. Derrida refers to these contradictory elements as alterity, or oth-erness. Frequently, they represent the voices of the powerless or neglected or overlooked members of society. The illusory unity must be negated, by allowing the disenfranchised to speak.[7]

There is another way in which Derrida expresses his hostil-ity to omni-inclusive systems. He distinguishes between the engineer and the *bricoleur,* a French word meaning something like a handyman or do-it-yourselfer. The engineer works with precision, with blueprints and schematic diagrams, with surveys and tests and the like. His work has a systematic quality. The bricoleur, on the other hand, makes do with what he finds at hand. He manages to fit things together, not always in an exact fashion, but by adjusting things, trimming off a little here and there. He does not always work from a precise plan, but works in a trial-and-error manner. This, says Derrida, is much more how the deconstructionist philosopher is. Reality does not really present itself as fully coherent. By its very nature it seems to be irregular and mottled.[8]

Foucault also observes this tendency to suppress contrary voices, but he emphasizes the persons more than the ideas that are subjugated. As we have observed, for Foucault the truth is that which is established by those who have the power to do so. In so doing, they intentionally ignore the potential contributions of others. Thus, for example, the doctor makes his diagnosis of the patient's condition and prescribes the remedy. While he consults the patient regarding what symptoms the latter is experiencing, the patient is not expected or allowed to diagnose or treat himself. The same is true of the psychiatrist and his or her client. And with the teacher and student, the student's ideas about what is true and what should be studied are largely ignored. Those in power make sure that those with contrary ideas are not heard. In some settings, this is done by the majority booing so loudly that opposing voices cannot be heard. What is happening is that those in power formulate their theory. They prevent contrary expressions, so that the theory seems unchallenged. On the basis of that view, then, they proceed to oppress the minority.

Although Foucault does not use this example, an excellent instance could be found in the dominance of communism in the middle to late twentieth century in the nations of Eastern Europe. On the basis of the theory of dialectical materialism, all contrary voices were suppressed by those in power. When people objected too emphatically, they were killed, imprisoned, or shipped off to a gulag. This treatment of individuals was justified on the basis that the individual was of little importance compared to the good of the group. The theory was maintained by preventing the expression of contrary considerations, and its apparently unanimous consent and self-evidence were regarded as justifying the suppression of those other voices and the oppression of minorities. Another example is the former practice of slavery in the United States. In many cases, slavery was justified in the minds of the ruling public by a view that whites were superior to blacks. To be sure, contrary opinions were held by the slaves, but their voices were not permitted public expression. They were forcibly restrained from such protest. In each of these cases, eventually the number of those expressing divergent understandings became sufficiently great that they could no longer be suppressed. To Foucault, this is the inherent problem with metanarratives. They have been used, historically, as means of oppression, and they will continue to be so used.

A strongly autobiographical element is at work in Richard Rorty's avoidance of metanarratives. He was raised in New York City by parents who were followers of the communist philosopher Leon Trotsky. The family also used to spend week-ends in the New Jersey countryside, and the young Rorty became interested in the wild orchids that grew there, becoming quite a student of them. As he grew older, he began looking for a system that would tie together into one scheme both his Trotskyite philosophy and the wild orchids. As an undergraduate philosophy student at the University of Chicago he continued to pursue this goal. Studying one after another of the philosophers, however, he observed how each had contradicted and refuted his predecessor's view. Rorty became convinced that the view of truth as being a statement's correspondence to observable reality was not workable, so he adopted instead the view that a philosophy is to be measured by how closely its tenets fit together logically. Yet he realized that those who prevailed on this measure of truth were those who were most skillful at drawing distinctions.

He finally concluded that it was impossible to devise a philosophy that summed up everything in a system. The pursuit that had been going on with great intensity since the time of Plato was futile. There was only one possibility of achieving such a synoptic vision, and that was not really an option for him: "I came to realize that the search of the philosophers for a grand scheme that would encompass everything was illusory. Only a theism that combined a God with equal measures of truth, love, and justice, could do the trick. But since I could not imagine myself being religious, and had indeed become more raucously secular, I did not consider that to be an option for me."[9] For Rorty, then, the objection to metanarratives or grand stories is not on quite the same basis as it is for Derrida and Foucault. He rejects metanarratives not so much for their adverse effects or the improper uses to which they have been put, but for the impossibility of a finite human being accomplishing such a feat.

Further, Rorty does not believe it necessary to have a big picture of things. Often, the big picture is given as a reason why one should engage in a course of action. For example, "why should I not murder?" "Because God has forbidden murder." Or, "why should I submit to military service, at the risk of possible death?" "Because it is for the good of the country, and ultimately, for the good of all the citizens of this country." Those who hold to a given big picture or complete story believe that if the big picture were abandoned, there would be no motivation for being good and moral, and morality would collapse. Similarly, it is the motivating and encouraging basis for and force behind many other aspects of life. For example, Christians are able to live resolutely in the face of great trials and sufferings because they believe the Christian story. It teaches them that God is watching over them and will preserve them, and that there is an eternity beyond this life, where rewards will be given for faithfulness.

Rorty does not, however, think it necessary to believe in any such big picture in order to maintain morality. Instead, he will simply substitute for the big picture such considerations as that it works out better. How does he know this is the case? Because a similar "big picture" argument was once made for the necessity of religious belief. Voltaire once said, "If there is no God, all is permitted," and many people agreed. Yet the decline of religious belief has not led to moral chaos and anarchy. Instead, people have substituted other bases. For example, concern for the welfare of one's grandchildren and their descendants has taken the place of belief in the future life in heaven.[10]

The Role of Community

One problem that arises in connection with the type of philosophy we have been examining is the potential for subjectivism. If there is no final, fixed meaning of texts based on a reality in the nature of things, and if the meaning emerges from a free play of language, may not the meaning for me be actually different than your meaning? How, then, can there be any agreement on the meaning of statements, or even any meaningful discussion of them? This has seemed to present a significant problem for postmodernists. The concept of community is believed to solve this problem, and one of the most vigorous advocates of this idea is Stanley Fish. A literature professor and literary critic, he is a representative of the so-called Yale school of literary criticism.

Probably Fish's best-known statement comes from an incident that contributes the title to one of his books. Fish tells of a student who came to one of his colleagues at the conclusion of the first day's session of a class and asked, "Is there a text in this class?" The professor immediately replied, "Yes; it's the *Norton Anthology of Literature.*" The student then responded, "No, I mean in this class do we believe in poems and things, or is it just us?"[11]

Fish realizes that some would use this incident to argue that once you depart from the literal meaning of a text, there is no real limitation on the meaning you might find in it. There might be as many meanings as there are readers. Actually, Fish claims, in the incident just recited there are *two* literal meanings of the student's question. One is that which it has in the circumstances the instructor assumed, namely, an inquiry about the required text-

51

book for the course. The other, which the question has in the circumstances the student assumed, was an inquiry regarding the professor's view of the text. Communication does not take place in a vacuum, but in the context of an institutional community. In such a context, one hears statements within an assumed set of purposes and intentions. Definite meaning does not derive from some fixed meaning embedded within a given text, but from the context of the interpretive community. Since both the student and the instructor are within that community, "their interpretive activities are not free, but what constrains them are the understood practices and assumptions of the institution and not the rules and fixed meanings of a language system."[12]

Some would contend that one of these meanings is the natural or obvious meaning of the statement, but Fish disagrees. Actually, he says, neither of these meanings would be immediately available to a native speaker of the language. Rather, the meaning that the instructor attached to the statement would only be apparent to someone familiar with what happens on the first day of a class. In fact, there are other possible meanings as well. The student's question ("Is there a text in this class?") might be understood as an inquiry about the location of an object, such as, "I think I left my book in this room. Have you seen it?" This does not mean that there are an infinite number of possible meanings, however, because there are constraints upon the possible meanings. The reality is that all sentences come embedded in some situation or other, which means that the statement has a particular meaning in that situation, although in other circumstances that meaning would be different. While some meanings are accessible to more people than are others, that is because more people are familiar with that situation, not because that is *the* only meaning of the text.

Some scholars, such as E. D. Hirsch, have contended that there are some statements that cannot really admit of more than one interpretation. They have a determinate meaning that everyone would agree upon. Hirsch proposes as an example the statement, "The air is crisp," which he believes anyone could see to be a statement about the weather. Actually, says Fish, this agreement is not because the statement is independent of any context. Rather, it is embedded in a context, in which most people hear it. There could be other contexts, such as a musical context: "When the piece is played correctly, the air is crisp."

Two conclusions follow from this discussion, Fish claims. First, there is not some meaning that words have in a normative linguistic system. Second, however, this does not mean that one is free to attach any meaning one wishes to the statement. There are constraints upon this meaning, constraints imposed by the situation in which the statement appears.

One might get the impression that there is a sort of two-stage process of interpretation. The first would be the hearing of the statement. Then, an interpretation is attached to it. Actually, says Fish, this is not the case. The actual hearing of the statement takes place within the situation, so that it is heard with a certain meaning.[13]

Rorty also places a great deal of importance on the role of community. He contends that one difference between the two types of philosophy we examined earlier is seen in two different ways people try to give life some sense by relating it to something larger than themselves. The traditional way is objectivism.

In this approach, one endeavors to relate one's ideas to some set of facts, some reality that exists. The other way, which Rorty advocates, is to seek connection with a community. On the former model, truth is understood as "correspondence with reality." On the latter model, truth is instead understood as "what is good for us now to believe." To say that something is not true is not to say that it does not fit the facts; it simply is to say that someone may at some point in the future come up with another idea, one that works better. On this model, objectivity would not be found in amassing more evidence for the view in question. Rather, it would involve widening the circle of agreement to the greatest possible extent.[14]

An example of this phenomenon can be seen by noting one of the features attending the extraordinary 2000 presidential election in the United States. With the electoral college count insufficient to elect either candidate, and the outcome of the election in the key state of Florida uncertain, some supporters of Vice President Gore contended that since he had a larger number of popular votes, he should be declared the winner. They argued that the popular vote should be the basis of election, not the vote within the electoral college, the United States Constitution notwithstanding. They sought to establish their position, basically by attempting to enlarge the circle of those who agreed, without amending the Constitution. This, it can be seen, was an attempt to resolve a disagreement by social agreement, not by an appeal to the existing law.

A Different Kind of Logic

A final theme among postmodern intellectuals is a reticence about the traditional type of logic. The logical pattern of thinking that most of us in the West use is not something about which we consciously reflect very often. It is like the grammar of our language. We simply use it without thinking about it, except in those few situations where we find ourselves in doubt. So in our thinking and speaking, we use logic without ordinarily being conscious of it. Only when we must deal with a puzzle of some type do we ask how something relates to something else. Nonetheless, we are using logic all the time.

Western logic was probably first worked out systematically by Aristotle. In deductive logic, there are three important principles: the law of identity, the law of contradiction (or noncontradiction), and the law of excluded middle. The law of identity simply means that A is A. So, for example, a tree is a tree. The law of contradiction means that something cannot be both A and not-A at the same time and in the same respect. So if something is a tree, it cannot also not be a tree. The law of excluded middle means that something is either A or not-A. It must be one or the other. This object is either a tree or not a tree. It cannot be something somewhere *between* a tree and not a tree. Different thinkers have interpreted differently the status of these logical principles. Some have regarded them as innate characteristics of the human mind. Others have considered them to be the structure of the universe. More theologically inclined persons have considered them to have been produced or authored by God, perhaps as being the very way God himself thinks. Regardless of the basis, most persons have tended to regard these logical principles or laws as essential to human thought and communication.

Derrida has challenged this common belief. He contends for an alternative logic. So, for example, he says, "It is thus not simply false to say that Mallarmé is a Platonist or a Hegelian. But it is above all not true. And vice versa."[15] He has not made much effort to elucidate exactly what he means by this statement. It appears that he is endeavoring to break down the dependence upon and trust in rational thought as the sole way of knowing. The effect of such a statement is to frustrate the mind's ability to absorb it, and to drive us to fall back upon our feelings. In this respect, it is much like the "koans" that Zen Buddhism has devised and employed. (Koans are questions such as, "You know the sound of two hands clapping; what is the sound of one hand clapping?") Zen Buddhism clearly rejects the purely rational approach to life, contending that paradoxes and contradictions are of the very nature of reality. As such, Derrida's alternative logic appears to be another form of postmodernism's reaction against the modern period's purely rational view of life and its elevation of the scientific method as the preferred model of knowing.

We have examined several major concepts that are present in the philosophy of postmodernism. It is important to understand that there are widely differing interpretations and assessments of the thoughts we have examined. Some understand the postmodernists to be saying something rather moderate. They are not seeking to eliminate all objective truth; they are simply arguing against the certainty, the finality, of such truth. Those who interpret postmodernist thought in this more conservative fashion can find passages in the writings of Derrida and Foucault, for example, in which they say something like this. Others, however, give a considerably more radical interpretation of postmodernism, according to which it much more completely undermines the concept of objective reality and objective truth. They also can cite passages that appear to justify this more radical interpretation. How, then, are we to decide among such conflicting understandings?

It may be helpful to consider the possibility that this conflict between different statements in postmodern writings is itself a key, or even *the* key, to understanding postmodernism. The very idea that if the "conservative" interpretation is true, the more radical one cannot be, assumes a traditional view of logic. Perhaps, however, within postmodernism this assumption does not hold true. There may not be anything remarkable, to a postmodernist, about saying two contradictory things, and that in itself indicates postmodernism's distinctiveness.

3

POSTMODERNISM
AND CHRISTIANITY

O ne question that will immediately arise for Christians is
how this mood and way of thinking relates to the
Christian faith. Is it possible to be a Christian and to be postmodern? Are there elements of postmodernism that are compatible with traditional Christianity, perhaps even conducive to
it, and are there elements that are in conflict with Christianity?

We must first ask, however, whether this is yet an issue. Are
there indications that Christianity, specifically evangelical
Christianity, has absorbed and is displaying any elements of
postmodernism? We will note a couple of anecdotes. While
anecdotal evidence does not establish anything by itself, I would
ask the reader to examine his or her own experience, and see
whether these incidents reflect something that rings true.

Indications of Postmodernism in Popular Christianity

An adult Sunday school class is working through a doctrinal
study book. In one lesson, the author suggests that the Pharisees
were not disciplined, and offers as support two passages from
the Gospels. Two women in the class object to the author's com-

ment, observing that in one of the passages, there is an emphasis upon the Pharisees' rigorous keeping of the law. They do not
think the verse supports what the author claims. Another member of the class reads from a different translation, which uses the
word *lawless* to describe the Pharisees. A seminary professor in
the class is asked his opinion. He says that he does not have a
Greek New Testament with him, but if the word is *anomia,* that
would support the idea that while the Pharisees were outwardly
very punctilious in following the law, they may have been
inwardly rebellious. The two women repeat their comment that
they don't think this verse applies, and the matter is dropped.

Here we have a popular Christian version of something we
discussed in the first chapter. The issue is not settled by appealing to the facts, or by consulting a more informed person, who
presumably would have better knowledge of those facts.
Rather, the feelings of a couple of persons that this does not fit
the issue are sufficient for them. And, as in so many cases of this
type, no effort is made to reach some sort of agreement as to
what the correct interpretation is. To do that would involve a
judgment that one interpretation is correct, and that another
therefore is not. That, however, would be a rejection of some
persons. Thus, in effect, any of several answers are accepted, not
because the evidence is insufficient to reach a conclusion but
because further effort is not made. So a practical pluralism or
relativism is practiced.

Let us examine one more case. A small denomination has
been debating a doctrinal issue, in particular, the legitimacy of
a specific position being taught by a professor at its denominational college. Two groups of pastors organize, one seeking

to amend the denominational statement of faith so that it will specifically exclude the professor's view, the other arguing for the legitimacy of that view. Finally, two resolutions are introduced. The first declares the traditional position of the denomination and of orthodox Christianity to be contrary to the professor's view. The second, presented by the other group of pastors, commends the professor as a valuable member of the college community and states that he should be allowed to continue to teach his view; however, certain restrictions are placed upon how he presents it. Both resolutions pass, by similar margins.

What has happened is that traditional logic has been suspended, since the wording of the two resolutions makes them contradictory. Having enabled the first group of pastors to "win" on their resolution, the delegates gave the second group what they wanted as well. It was a "win-win" situation, but actually was something of a "lose-lose" outcome. The second group of pastors, being of a somewhat more postmodern orientation, were much more satisfied with the outcome than were the pastors in the first group.

Symptoms of postmodernism can sometimes be found in strange places. We noted earlier the lack of concern for consistency of attire. Inconsistency of ideas or of belief and practice can also be noted. In one seminary, a group of students formed an informal organization to promote serious theological discussion. They were especially proud of their thoroughgoing Calvinism, a theology that holds that all that occurs is the result of God's plan and will. Yet without giving up this formal theology, they came to adopt a view of Christian decision-making that assumes that God does not have a specific plan for the Christian's life.

As we acknowledged, these cases are merely anecdotal and could be countered by using anecdotes that illustrate the contrary. There is, however, evidence of a somewhat more scientific nature that substantiates these experiences. The Barna organization has for some years conducted polls on religious and other topics, using samples carefully adjusted to reflect the general public. In a 1991 poll they presented the statement, "There is no such thing as absolute truth; different people can define truth in conflicting ways and still be correct," and asked for a response of agreement, disagreement, strong agreement, strong disagreement, or uncertainty. Interestingly, a majority of those who identified themselves as born-again Christians and a majority of those who considered themselves evangelical Christians either agreed or strongly agreed with that statement, suggesting a belief in the relativity of truth.[1] Although there was some ambiguity, so that there might simply have been agreement with the idea that there are differences of interpretation, this conclusion cannot simply be disregarded.

A 1992 Barna poll indicated a rather high degree of correct understanding of the basis of salvation. When asked to describe their belief about life after death, 62 percent of the general sample correctly responded, "When you die, you will go to heaven because you have confessed your sins and have accepted Jesus Christ as your Savior." Only 6 percent said, "When you die you will go to heaven because you have tried to obey the Ten Commandments," 9 percent said, "because you are basically a good person," and 6 percent said, "because God loves all people and will not let them perish."[2] When asked to respond to the statement, "All good people, whether they consider Jesus Christ to be their Savior or not, will live in heaven after they die on earth," 25 percent of those who said they had made a personal commitment to Jesus Christ (which in turn comprised 65 percent of the total adult sample) agreed strongly and 15 percent agreed moderately; 16 percent disagreed moderately and 33 percent disagreed strongly; 11 percent did not know. Thus, of those who would hazard an opinion, those who disagreed outnumbered those who agreed by less than a 5 to 4 ratio! Even 29 percent of the born-again and 26 percent of the Baptists agreed, either strongly or somewhat. It appears that while a strong majority agree in theory on what qualifies a person for entrance into heaven, when the question shifts to who will actually get there, a very different view is taken by a significant portion of the sample. Probably the emotional factor has overwhelmed the rational.

This is etiquette, concern for the feelings of others, and what has happened is that etiquette has become more important than ethics today. In this sort of environment it is a serious breach of etiquette to accuse someone of having told an untruth. This would be the case even if the person in question has actually told an untruth. To accuse someone of committing an improper act is disapproved of more strongly than the actual committing of such an act.

Relating Christianity to Changing Times

Over the years of church history, Christians have held several different opinions about how they should relate their Christian beliefs to the spirit of the times. Some contend that not only what is believed, but also the particular way of expressing it must be preserved. No adaptation of the presentation of the Christian message in light of the cultural situation of the recipient(s) is needed. One simply declares the message, relying upon the Holy Spirit to make it intelligible. Similarly, as cultural forces change, there is no need to alter the way one understands the doctrines or explains them to oneself.

A second group believes that there is an unchanging content of the Christian faith. Unless this content is preserved, we are no longer dealing with what could be termed Christianity. In this respect, this group is similar to the first one described above. Unlike them, however, these Christians believe that the form of conception or expression of the message can appropriately be adapted to suit the situation and the times. Just as the Bible can be translated into many different languages without changing what it says, so its message can be expressed in many different cultural forms without losing the essential meaning of the original. So it can be brought forth in various time periods, using ways of thinking current at those times. Similarly, it can be expressed in different cultures, including African and Asian, just as it is in Western or First World ways of thinking. It can also be expressed at different levels of sophistication and abstractness or complexity. It can be put in language and imagery understandable by children, or that which makes sense to a highly educated adult.

Issues at Risk for Christianity

It does appear that Christianity has a major stake in the outcome of the discussions posed by postmodernism. One aspect of this pertains to the conception of truth. The Scripture writers claim that there is an objective truth. Again and again this fact is asserted, sometimes in rather small matters, sometimes in much larger issues. For example, following Jesus' resurrection, the apostle Thomas had rather serious doubts about its reality, since he had not been present with the other disciples when they saw Jesus. He declared, "Unless I see the nail marks in his hands and put my finger where the nails were, and put my hand into his side, I will not believe it" (John 20:25). Jesus then appeared to him and the other disciples, and specifically invited Thomas to see his hands and to place his hand in the wound in his side. Jesus' claim that he really was alive and was the same person who had been with them earlier could be tested factually. It was not sufficient simply to have the subjective feeling that Jesus was all right and was with the disciples. Rather, this was a space-time matter that could be established by sense experience. This was, presumably, the type of thing that anyone could have verified if they were willing to fulfill the conditions, namely, of being there and examining Jesus' body.

Another case is John the Baptist. In prison, John began to wonder if he had been following the right person, or whether someone else was the messiah. So he sent his disciples to Jesus to ask this question. The answer was not in an authoritarian statement, "Yes, I am he!" Rather, Jesus pointed out the things that were happening in his ministry: "The blind receive sight, the lame walk, those who have leprosy are cured, the deaf hear, the dead are raised, and the good news is preached to the poor" (Luke 7:22). These were objective facts, which any observer could verify, and which then could be reported to others.

Now it might well be objected that this was really a pragmatic matter, rather than a question of correspondence with the facts. The belief in Jesus' deity worked out well for those who believed: they were healed or received other major benefits from Jesus. Note, however, that on another level, it is the objective fact, the correspondence of the belief to the actual state of affairs, which underlies the claim that this has "worked out."

Further, this objective or correspondence type of truth does not find its objectivity simply in a language in which the meaning is built up through a "free play" of words. Rather, this truth is rooted in or based on a rationality that exists prior to and independent of any human individual's discovery or recognition of it. God speaks, and what he says comes to pass. Indeed, to the extent that knowledge is the discovery of the way the world is, it is the discovery of the structure God has placed within it, for he has created all that is, and just as it is. The opening words of the Bible declare that "God created the heavens and the earth," a Hebrew idiom expressing the idea of everything that exists. So there is a basis for truth, independent of individual or group knowers of it. This basis is not simply in the visible system of nature. It goes beyond that to the One who is the source, preserver, and guarantor of the whole great universe.

How does this relate to the postmodern view of truth? Depending upon the variety of postmodernism one is considering, the understanding of truth may frequently be quite different. In particular, Derrida's rejection of logocentrism and metaphysics of presence directly conflicts with the biblical picture of truth. His understanding is that truth is not simply some external, preexistent reality, waiting there for us to discover (metaphysics of presence), but something that we build up by the free play of language. On that basis, there could be no god, or if there is a god, he is someone who has no real effect upon the truth that we find. Consequently, it appears that Christians, who want to preserve the full scope of Christianity, must be prepared to resist and reject such a view of truth.

What, however, about the nature of the text? Is meaning something that resides within the text, so that the task of hermeneutics is, as the word *exegesis* would suggest, to find that meaning and lead it out of the text? On such a model, the meaning is there, independent of the reader, and is unaffected by changing circumstances or time. In the case of the Scriptures, that meaning is there because God has revealed himself and has inspired the Scripture writers to record accurately what he has revealed. The nature of prophecy is that what God has declared will come to pass, regardless of how people interpret or believe it. Here again there seems to be a conflict between traditional or evangelical Christianity and the postmodern treatment of a topic on which their interest coincides.

One of the most conspicuous features of Christianity is that it does present a metanarrative. That is to say, it is a universal explanation, and in two respects. It is universal or all-inclusive, in the sense of tying together everything, all aspects or elements of reality. It is also universal in the sense that it is a narrative that claims to be valid for absolutely all members of the human race. It is not simply a local narrative, or the story of one segment of the human race. The creation account tells the story of the entire human race. Adam and Eve are the one pair from whom all humans are descended. The explanation of the universal fact of sin and the universal need of salvation is that Adam sinned as the head of the race and thus implicated all humans in his guilt. Further, in the judgment scene in the Bible (Matt. 25:31-46) all persons, from all segments of the human race, are gathered together.

The God who is the center of the Christian message is exclusive. God insists that he is the only true and living God, and consequently, he will tolerate no worship of or commitment to any other claimed deity (Ex. 20:3). The divided loyalty of the Hebrew people is rebuked, and the challenge of a claimant, Baal, is tested at Mount Carmel (1 Kings 18:20-40). There Jehovah establishes his exclusive rights, by sending down fire in response to Elijah's prayers, in contrast to the futile requests of the priests of Baal. The reason that the people are to worship only Jehovah is that he is the only real God, and has demonstrated this to be the case.

Further, there is only one way of proper approach to this one true God. Both Jesus and his disciples made it very clear that the only way to come to God is through Jesus Christ. This is true for everyone, not merely those of a particular culture or nationality. Thus, there is an exclusiveness to the truth, and only one way to obtain the way of life that Christianity promises.

Christianity maintains that there is an objective authority for humans. Much of postmodernism has rejected the idea of an external God who has the right to prescribe what is right and what is true. To the postmodernist, this appears to be an imposition of power on human beings. Thus, the authority of the church, the Bible, or the clergy must be thrown off. Truth and morality are simply what a community decides they are. Christianity, however, insists that God is the infinite One, and that humans must submit themselves to his will.

Contrast this, then, with the pluralism that is so much a part of postmodernism. There, the truth is plural, because everyone is subject to the limitations of historical and cultural conditioning. A given religious faith is "true" for a given person, if he or she perceives life and reality this way. The various religions have arisen in given settings, and their apparent self-evidence is simply due to the fact that those who hold them have not really been exposed to any other ways of thinking, or if they have, those other ways have seemed so strange or alien that they were not real options for those people.

Finally, the Christian faith includes a strong emphasis on the objectivity of moral standards. The principles that underlie the divine commands are not merely arbitrary, nor applicable only to a small group of persons. They are not simply the standards agreed on by a given community for its members. They are objectively good, based on God's will and decree, which in turn come from his very nature. In contrast, postmodernism is opposed to any sort of natural law ethic, or any transcendent basis in the Good. Like truth, good is something that must be worked up. It is that which the community establishes as its working rules, like the rules of the road. It is what works out well for those who practice it. Here is another irreconcilable conflict between postmodernism and traditional Christian belief and practice.

Preserving the Substance of the Christian Message

Yet the reality is that, despite these points of conflict between the two, the postmodern world exists, and Christians must be concerned to live relevantly in that world and to relate the Christian message to it. How then shall we seek to relate this message?

I find it helpful to distinguish between the *substance* of the Christian message and the *style* of its ministry or presentation — between the *content* and the *form* of the message. One approach says that the content of the message must be adapted to fit the situation. This may involve simply attempting to modify the style, but to such an extent that the content or the substance becomes altered in the process. Or it may occur simply through so deemphasizing a particular element of the message that it becomes functionally modified. An example, not necessarily exclusive to this context, is the doctrine of sin. While few if any Christians have actually abandoned belief in this traditional doctrine of Christianity, there has been a considerable muting of that motif, out of a desire not to offend the hearer. The result, however, of not mentioning the doctrine is that the other elements of the message are developed in its absence. Thus, it has no real effect upon the total message.

It is sometimes difficult to determine when one is saying the same thing in a different way, and when one is actually saying something with a different meaning. In the first third of the twentieth century, one powerful voice of liberalism, or "theological modernism," was Harry Emerson Fosdick. He insisted that what must be done is to retain the fundamental experiences, but to give them new or updated ideological expressions. So, for example, he took the doctrine of the second coming. That, he declared, could no longer be held in its literal form. What we must do is isolate the experience that underlies this doctrine, and Fosdick believed that to be the experience of hope. What form of teaching could we use that would preserve this experience, but without the obsolete trappings of the doctrine of the second coming? Fosdick believed he found this expression in the belief in progress, although not of inevitable progress.

Is this really preserving the original content, however? Even if thinking simply in terms of the experience, it appears to me that there is a significant difference in the experience involved in the two ideas. The experience attached to the idea of the second coming is that of the triumph of God, through his working, which might come out of a situation in which things had deteriorated. The idea of progress, on the other hand, although Fosdick was careful to avoid reducing this to inevitable progress, is nonetheless considerably broader and more inclusive than is the idea of the second coming. It could involve a less supernatural basis than the second coming, and does include the idea of progressive improvement. As such, it would be more conducive to the postmillennial view than to other ideas of the second coming. What had happened was that Fosdick had smuggled in, without our awareness and perhaps even without his, a specific form of teaching. It is our judgment, therefore, that in this case the change involves not only the style or form, but also the substance or content.

But, one might ask, is it really important to preserve the content? Is Christianity that content-oriented a religion? There are numerous places in Scripture where the importance of the content or doctrine believed is emphasized. We have already noted the emphasis in the Ten Commandments, the contest on Mount Carmel, and elsewhere, of relating to the right God. This means in part, however, having the right understanding of God. In his famous speech to the Areopagus, Paul dealt with people who were very religious, who definitely believed in a god of some sort. Yet he insisted that their belief in the unknown god was not sufficient, and he proceeded to declare that unknown god to them. This included the information that this god had created the world, and had set the times and boundaries of nations. Most specifically, however, Paul referred to the One whom this God had appointed, and indicated that a time was coming when God would judge the world by this One whom he had appointed, and that in fact he had raised him from the dead (Acts 17:34).

The same is true of beliefs about Jesus. At one point in his ministry, Jesus asked his disciples who people were saying that he was. The disciples reported the varying opinions they had heard: John the Baptist, Elijah, Jeremiah, or one of the prophets. Then, however, Jesus asked them for their own opinion, or more correctly, their own conviction. Speaking for the disciples, Peter declared: "You are the Christ, the Son of the living God" (Matt. 16:16). At this point Jesus praised Peter and, through him, the rest of the disciples, and entrusted certain authority and power to them. It appears that his doing so was dependent upon his having determined that the disciples' understanding and belief were correct.

But certainly, we might suggest, it is sufficient to believe in the deity and humanity of Jesus, and to allow variations in the understanding of what these doctrines mean. Arianism taught that Jesus was a god, the highest of the created beings; Apollinarianism proposed that Jesus had a human body but only a divine psyche; and Eutychianism held that Jesus had only one nature, a hybrid of deity and humanity. Should these be allowable variations for the sake of relating to a specific situation? Here it is interesting to notice how John dealt with a similar case. The problem that apparently was vexing some of the churches at the time John wrote his first letter was something called docetism. The word is derived from the Greek word that means to "seem" or to "appear." These people believed fully in the deity of Jesus, but they had some questions about his humanity. In its fully developed form, docetism was the teaching that Jesus' supposed humanity was only an appearance. John's reply was firm and clear: "This is how you can recognize the Spirit of God: Every spirit that acknowledges that Jesus Christ has come in the flesh is from God, but every spirit that does not acknowledge Jesus is not from God. This is the spirit of the antichrist, which you have heard is coming and even now is already in the world" (1 John 4:2-3). John referred to those who denied Christ's full humanity as "false prophets" (v. 1).

Another place in Scripture where retention of the exact form of teaching is insisted upon is in Paul's discussion of the resurrection of Christ in 1 Corinthians 15. Here he makes very clear how important it is that the Corinthians believe in the resurrection. Without that, their faith is empty, and his preaching is empty as well (v. 17). He struggles with how to communicate the nature of the resurrection body, which he describes as a "spiritual body" (v. 44), and its exact relationship to the body that dies and is buried. Yet he makes it clear that the body is raised (vv. 35-49). Where some would soon claim that the coming of Christ and the resurrection were simply spiritual, not bodily and physical, Paul holds to a definite resurrection of the body that has died.

Paul also insisted upon the correct understanding of grace. Some might be inclined to see salvation as of grace, but as also requiring some measure of works to complete it. In the letter to the Galatians, Paul addressed such views. He strongly identified the view of the Judaizers, who were proposing the need to observe the law, as being "a different kind of gospel" (1:8-9). He was unequivocal in his denunciation of such a person: "let him be eternally condemned" (v. 9).

The Inevitability of Conflict

It is worth noticing that at several points Scripture indicates a fundamental conflict between Christianity's teachings and non-Christian views of reality. This is often put in terms of the relationship between the things of Christ and the things of the world. One of the most pointed of these is found in Paul's opening statements in First Corinthians. He begins the discussion by saying: "For the message of the cross is foolishness to those who are perishing, but to us who are being saved it is the power of God" (1 Cor. 1:18). He goes on to say that God will destroy the wisdom of the wise and frustrate the intelligence of the intelligent (v. 19). Paul specifies this somewhat further by stating that the Jews demand miraculous signs and the Greeks seek for wisdom (v. 22), and makes quite clear that these will not be provided. In particular, the crucified Christ is a stumbling block to Jews and foolishness to Gentiles (v. 23). God had chosen persons who did not have great distinction within society. There were few influential persons or persons of noble birth (v. 26). Paul's own ministry had been in weakness and fear, not in great human wisdom or learning or eloquent speech (2:3-4). This was so that their faith might not rest on human wisdom, but on the power of God (2:5). Nonetheless, the message that Paul and his fellow evangelists have been proclaiming to the Corinthians has a kind of wisdom of its own, but a divine wisdom, which has been hidden but now has been revealed by God (vv. 6-7, 10). This is so that faith would not be a product of human wisdom, in which case persons could have boasted in their accomplishments (1:28-29; 2:5, 8-9).

Passages like this, if taken seriously, lead us to the realization that there will always be some point of conflict or disagreement between the Christian message and any current human philosophy. We should therefore expect to find that we cannot simply make Christianity completely compatible with postmodernism, or completely postmodernize Christianity, without thereby distorting the Christian message to some extent. In this, the relationship of Christianity to its surrounding culture today is no different than its relationship to the culture of any other period. In other words, just as there cannot be a completely postmodern Christianity, there cannot be a completely modern Christianity either. Nor can there be a perfect amalgamation of the Christian message with the ideology of any coming period. There will always be something of a tension between Christianity and the spirit of any age.

Consequently, we must be cautious about aligning our Christian belief too closely with any human philosophy. It is not uncommon for evangelicals who are trying to make their theology postmodern to point out the mistakes of evangelicals of an earlier period, of too closely identifying with modernism. In some cases, this was done consciously, and the actual content of the modern worldview was accepted, with a consequent alteration of the content of Christian theology. These were the persons who actually became theological modernists or liberals. Others, however, while rejecting the tenets of modernism, adopted the intellectual framework, the categories, the way of reasoning and judging, which were characteristic of modernism. While remaining evangelicals in what they believed, they became modernists in the way they reasoned. Their theology therefore contained an inherent contradiction and eventually, if not modified, would have ended up having a modern content, if the modern age had not gone into decline. In this respect, they would have been like the apologists who adopted Enlightenment assumptions and eventually became victims of a type of deism. The underlying assumption that the tenets of belief could be demonstrated by reason became transformed into the view that unless they could be so demonstrated they should be abandoned. If we are to learn from the past, we should also be wary of the idea that a too thorough postmodernizing of the faith can be engaged in, without thereby also distorting the faith. Like the Trojan horse, taking the contemporary worldview into one's faith may lead to a fatal destruction of what one would preserve.

It may be argued by some, however, that what we have described is not such a serious matter. If it is the case that each set of beliefs sooner or later has to be abandoned, is that all bad? May it perhaps be that Christianity is not a matter of fixed, permanent, unchanging ideas? Perhaps it is a living matter, which takes on different shapes at different times. Here we refer back to the earlier statements that indicate a declaration by biblical writers that there is a finality to the Christian message, and that it cannot be changed without altering the very character of Christianity.

Note carefully what we are saying here. Our argument is not

necessarily, at this point, that Christianity is true and that post-modernism is false. Rather, we are simply claiming that Christianity and many elements of postmodernism are different. It might be that postmodernism is correct, or more nearly correct than Christianity, but it is sufficiently different that thoroughly postmodern Christianity should no longer be termed Christianity. In this respect, our contention is similar to that of J. Gresham Machen, in his book *Christianity and Liberalism*, written nearly eight decades ago. He essentially argued that liberalism might be true, but that it was not Christianity and did not deserve to be known by that name.[3]

One test to see whether Christianity and postmodernism are compatible is to ask both sides in the discussion their view of this question. Notably, more enthusiastically postmodern Christians think that an amalgamation of the two is possible, and even desirable. To them, modernism is the enemy, the perverter, and postmodernism the ally to deliver Christianity from the dangers of modernism. To be sure, some Christians most emphatically reject postmodernism as an option, but it is not those that we are considering at this point. I have observed that if you ask each of two parties in a dispute to describe the other's view, the views they describe usually seem far apart. If, however, you ask each to describe his own view, the views seem much closer. In this case, however, we have an interesting phenomenon. Postmodern Christians consider the two views to be much closer than do postmodern non-Christians. The problem is especially intense in terms of the question of metanarratives, or the universal applicability of any worldview, in this case the worldview of Christianity. In the conflict between modern thought and

Christianity, both parties believed in the possibility, the desirability, perhaps even the necessity, of a universal explanation of life and reality. They differed, of course, as to what that universal explanation was to be, whether Christianity on the one hand, or scientific naturalism, dialectical materialism, Freudian psychoanalysis, or some other secular view on the other. In the present conflict, the difference is over whether a universal explanation or a metanarrative is even possible. I would contend that the universal element in the Christian message, the claim that there is one God, one creator, one ruler of the human race, is so deeply embedded in the testimony of the biblical documents that it cannot be wrenched from Christianity without destroying the very organism. While postmodern evangelical Christians may think the marriage with postmodernism is possible, most non-Christian postmodernists do not share that sanguine understanding of the interrelationship.

The Possibility of Dialogue

But is it possible for two views that claim to be so diverse in their orientations and their specific content to interact with one another? May it not be that they are so foreign to one another that no real conversation between the two is possible? Indeed, this is what postmodernists have contended. They would say that every attempt to understand their view is a misunderstanding. All attempts at some objective, neutral statement are inevitably mitigated by the fact that we are all historically and temporally conditioned. If this is the case, then it follows logically that, as the postmodern insists, there is no neutral ground into which two discussants can enter to debate or even to discuss the differences between their two views. The two dialogue partners are like two persons who meet, neither of whom knows the other's language or any third, common language shared by both. Add to this the idea that no interpreter is present, no one who is fluent in both languages who can mediate between the two, and you have a situation analogous to that between the modernist and the postmodernist, or between the Christian and the non-Christian postmodernist. How can they proceed?

It is worth observing that in practice neither party seems to hold to this consistently, or to practice the theory that is espoused. At least the postmodernist insists that one cannot understand postmodernism from a non-postmodern perspective. What is interesting, however, is that the postmodernist seems to believe that the non-postmodernist understands what he (the postmodernist) is saying when he tells him that he does not understand his statement of postmodernism. Here may be a preliminary insight. Is it possible that, when two persons who follow different patterns talk about patterns of thinking, they are not speaking in different patterns, or paradigms, as they are often called? Logically, it would seem that what must happen, if there is indeed to be communication of some kind, is that either one or the other must adopt the paradigm of the other, or that there is a common paradigm for such discussion, or that at the secondary level — the level of discussing paradigms — there are not differing paradigms.

Now let us return to our illustration and ask what actually happens when two people who do not understand a common language try to converse, and there is no translator present. What happened, for example, when the first Europeans came to

North America and encountered the native Americans? How did communication between them occur?

I suggest that what typically happens in such a situation is that communication begins at a nonlinguistic level. It begins with some common experience, and each then seeks to label or identify that experience with his or her own language. For example, take a native German who speaks only German, and an Englishman who speaks only English. Perhaps a dog is present. The Englishman may touch or point to the dog and say, "Dog." The German responds by saying, "Hund." Now they have one object regarding which they can communicate. Whenever the German utters the word "Hund" (at least when speaking literally), the Englishman knows that he is referring to what the Englishman means when he says "dog." This activity then progresses so that the relative sphere of common linguistic understanding is enlarged. Gradually, each man comes to know more of the other person's vocabulary. Verbs, adjectives, and abstract nouns are, of course, more difficult to learn on this model, but it can be accomplished, with some effort and a considerable amount of trial and error. Not only is this how persons learn each other's language. I would suggest that this is roughly how each of us came to learn our native language, by a process of observation, identification, and imitation.

I propose that this is how discussion of differing paradigms and from different paradigms proceeds as well. Without having thought about the nature of truth, there is a level on which there is a common understanding of the nature of truth. It is on this level that discussion must take place. It is common in philosophical circles to talk about correspondence, coherence, and pragmatic theories of truth. Actually, these are not so much conceptions of truth as they are tests of truth. They are ways of measuring whether a given idea or set of ideas is true, but all assume a similar fundamental conception of what truth really is. Basic to all of these theories is a common, prereflective conception of truth that I would call "primitive correspondence." By that, I mean that all of them are working with an idea that a statement is true if it fits with or correctly describes the way things are. I believe I can show this using a few quick examples.

Derrida claims that meaning is not simply "out there," objectively vested in something external to us, ready to be discovered and understood. Yet, interestingly, when philosopher John Searle wrote an eleven-page critique of Derrida's thought, the latter responded with a ninety-two-page rebuttal. One recurrent theme throughout the article is that Searle has misunderstood and misrepresented what Derrida was really saying.[4] Note that Searle's statement, on Derrida's contention, was false because it did not correctly describe the state of affairs, specifically, the meaning that Derrida intended when he wrote those words. Similarly, Rorty argues for a view of truth, not as mirroring the world, but as what works out. Yet, the question of what works out depends upon certain criteria of working out, and the issue of which is the better statement depends upon an assessment of certain states of affairs. Did such and such actually result? Is this what happened? At this level, there is a conception that truth is measured by results, but what is the measure of results?

There is yet another level on which this phenomenon can be observed. In ordinary, everyday experiences of social interaction, all persons, even postmodernists, rely upon a conception of truth as the way things are. When the postmodernist is stopped by a police officer for speeding, the discussion that follows does not assume, on either side, that the truth may be relative to the person uttering the statement. The question is whether the automobile was moving at a speed exceeding the limit, and the most objective measures possible are introduced to attempt to settle the question. Similarly, a postmodernist, checking out of a supermarket or a discount store, may have a discussion with the checkout person as to how many of a given item he has, but neither believes that the truth is relative to the person making the contention, although the self-interest of each person might tend toward quite different answers.

The upshot of what we are saying is this: human society assumes a common basis of reference, and a common, sufficiently neutral area of experience, so that there can be communication, persuasion, and rebuttal. Thus, there is a possibility of some sort of criticism of postmodernism that does not simply tacitly assume its contradictory as the criterion of evaluation.

It may now be necessary to go back and modify somewhat our illustration of the two persons who speak neither each other's language nor some common third language. There are some languages that are sufficiently similar to each other that native speakers of each can understand, at least in part, what a person speaking the other language is saying. Swedes and Norwegians, for example, can communicate to some extent, as can Spaniards and Portuguese. This is because their languages are part of the same language family. Perhaps this is a more accurate picture of the relationship between postmodernism and traditional Christianity than we sometimes think it to be.

Beyond what we have said, I would assert that all human discussion assumes as well a common kind of logic. It has been cus-
tomary to insist upon a type of logic in which a statement and its
contradictory could not both be true at the same time and in the
same respect. The usual way of putting it is to say that something
cannot be both A and not-A at the same time and in the same
respect. Derrida, in particular, has claimed to be using an alternative logic, one in which such oppositions are not necessarily
determinative. Whether this is the intention and the motivation
of such a position, it appears that in practice he and some other
postmodernists use this as a means of dodging criticisms. This
is done by making, in different places, statements on a given
issue that actually contradict one another. When one of these
statements is criticized, the postmodernist then cites a statement
of the opposing stance, thus contending that the criticism is
unjustified or unfair.

Is this really feasible, however? Do postmodernists actually
function on such a basis? I could point out numerous indications
that they do not. The very attempt to criticize differing viewpoints assumes the validity of the law of contradiction. For if this
is not the case, then any evidence or argument marshaled against
the other is of no avail; for although it may be indisputable, that
is of no consequence, for the contradictory can also be true.
When the deconstructionist speaks intellectually, he or she
appears to be asserting something in such a way as to exclude its
contradictory.

In fact, one cannot really function and does not function outside the theoretical realm in this way. A postmodernist who held
that a poisonous substance can be at the same time and in the

same respect nonpoisonous, and who lived life on such a basis, would have a relatively short life. And, as Dallas Willard asserts,[5] even the most relativistic, subjectivistic, and postmodern academic suddenly becomes very modern when issues like faculty benefits are discussed. Such a person does not really hold that his position on what benefits should be given and the administration's position are equally valid.

On one occasion, I was making this very point about logic in an academic paper. One of the scholars present, who had lived for a number of years in China, objected that the Chinese do not follow such a rigid system of logic. They do not require that only one of a pair of contradictories could be true. This, however, did not square with what I had experienced of Chinese persons functioning on a practical level. The thousands of bicyclists I saw in Beijing seemed to understand that a car cannot both be and not be in a particular spot at a particular time, and if they had not, they would not have remained alive. Beyond that, I realized that if a Chinese were asked whether my analysis of the Chinese understanding was correct, I could not be wrong. If the Chinese said yes, then of course I was right by concession. If, however, he said no, it would presumably be because there was a contradiction between his understanding and my understanding of it, in which case my position would also be demonstrated to be true.

All of us use such a logic, at least implicitly, when we make assertions of any kind. In particular, we do so when we object to any assertion. Society's very social functioning requires this. In the cases we cited earlier, not only was there an appeal to the "facts of the case" as to who was right (e.g., the police officer or the driver), but there was an assumption that they could not both be right. Views that contend that the laws of logic do not apply are usually doing one or more of several things. They are either arguing that certain areas are unique, not being bound by logic the way other areas are; or they are asserting that the issue of the truth in this case cannot be determined — that we simply cannot obtain, or to this point have not succeeded in obtaining, the relevant information to make this judgment. Or perhaps they are referring to situations that are ambiguous, or that need further specification. I have in mind here such issues as whether a given object is blue in color or green.

Human communication requires such a logic. Beyond that, however, even human thought requires it. If contradictories can really both be true, then it is not possible to think by distinguishing ideas from one another. I have a T-shirt that I bought from the American Philosophical Association, of which I am a member. On the front is printed the following: "The sentence on the back of this shirt is false." On the back, however, this appears: "The sentence on the front of this shirt is true." Now it may be possible to believe either the front or the back of the shirt, or to believe both, but at different times. It is not psychologically possible to believe both at the same time, and in the same respect. It simply cannot be done, while retaining one's sanity.

The problem is that to do so in effect would be to believe in the falsity of what one believes to be true. In a sense, it really is not possible for a person to believe that he is in error, for as soon as he realizes he is in error, he no longer believes what he believed, and thus is no longer in error. In a sense, one can only hold, "I *was* in error." For it is psychologically impossible for a sane person to think: "I believe this, and it is wrong," or "I know that what I truly believe is untrue."

What we have said does not in any sense establish Christianity's truth. It does, however, argue that it is possible for advocates of postmodernity and those of a non-postmodern viewpoint to communicate with one another and to evaluate the adequacy of competing viewpoints. It is to this issue of evaluation that we turn in the following chapter.

4

POSTMODERNISM:
GOOD, BAD,
OR INDIFFERENT?

What shall we make of postmodernism? Is it basically a correct and helpful way of understanding life? If so, then we should embrace it, regardless of whether it accords with our previous beliefs. If, on the other hand, it is an inaccurate view of reality and of life, then we should resist it and reject it.

As with virtually any understanding of thought or life, post-modernism has both strengths and weaknesses. We need to appreciate and utilize the strengths, but with due recognition of its shortcomings. We noted earlier that both more conservative and more radical interpretations are possible, even of the same postmodernist. To the extent that one follows the more conservative interpretation of postmodernism, it is less vulnerable to criticism, but it also is less unique. The same valid insights can be found in other philosophies that do not go as far. On the other hand, the more radical readings of postmodernism preserve its uniqueness, but make it more vulnerable to criticism. One can legitimately adopt either interpretation of postmodernism, but one cannot hold both, at least not without the loss of one's intellectual integrity.

Positive Elements of Postmodernism

Postmodernism offers certain strengths and accurate analyses, and we need to take note of them lest we miss their benefits. One of postmodernism's helpful and correct insights is that it is not possible to be absolutely certain about any system of thought. While we may possess absolute truth, it is quite a different matter to say that we understand it absolutely. Because of our human limitations, our beliefs will always contain an element of the uncertain and the merely probable. This, of course, should not be surprising, since Paul said that "we live by faith, not by sight" (2 Cor. 5:7). In particular, postmodernism's criticism of classical foundationalism seems to be correct. Foundationalism, especially in the tradition of the seventeenth-century French philosopher René Descartes, had sought for certitude by contending that there are certain unquestionable truths. These truths serve as the basis of all other knowledge claims, which can be derived from these foundations by deductive certainty. Thus, the conclusions are those about which one need, and indeed can, have no doubt.

We now know that what seemed so certain and indubitable to an earlier period is not that at all. The starting point of those systems turns out not to be inescapable, but rather to be of the nature of assumptions, or to contain hidden and unexpressed premises. Descartes, for example, believed that he started with an absolutely certain premise: I am doubting. Although he could doubt everything else, he could not doubt that he was doubting.

We now see, however, that Descartes' supposedly intuitive starting point was actually an inference from his experience, plus a suppressed premise. All he could really have properly said at the starting point was "Doubting is occurring." Anything more than that was an inference. Similar problems can be found with all other claimed foundationalisms. Whether the entire search for sure foundations has been discredited, every claimant to that task is seen to be fallible. It simply is not possible, either logically or psychologically, to expect that any rational person, willing to take the time to examine the evidence, must come to the same conclusion.

Second, the postmodernists have correctly pointed out that all of our knowledge is conditioned. Each of us functions from some particular point, where what we see and how we judge it is affected by our situation in time and place. All of our experiences, all that we have been exposed to in life, affects our judgment. Much of this is on an unconscious or preconscious level. This means that even the choice of issues to discuss is affected by the when and where of the discussion. An illustration of this can be seen in the discussions of pre- and postmillennialism, which flourished in conservative Christian circles in the first half of the twentieth century but now receive relatively little attention, although there are discussions (such as the theonomy debate) that embody similar underlying principles. The origin of humans was not a large topic of debate, either in the church or even in broader society, until the publication of Charles Darwin's *Origin of Species* and similar works on evolution.

Beyond that, however, the view of given issues is affected by our setting. Just how dramatic this can be is seen in the different reactions to the O. J. Simpson murder trial verdict on the part of whites and African-Americans. The conflicting testimonies by persons who witnessed the same event also underscore this truth. Who we are, how we have been educated, the societal sub-group that we have occupied are all very influential in how we see and understand things.

Our attitudes are affected and structured by our experiences. For example, my ability to think objectively about the Democratic party is still somewhat influenced by the fact that I lived in the city of Chicago in the late 1950s and early '60s. Many people familiar with the activities of the Cook County Democratic machine in those days believe that Richard Nixon probably won the presidential election in 1960, and the deciding state was Illinois. The closeness of the vote and the widely exposed voting irregularities in that county in those days con-tributes to such a belief.

Much of this kind of effect occurs on an unconscious level. Who, for example, living and functioning within a Protestant church today, can read the book of Romans without being influ-enced by the fact that Martin Luther lived, taught, and wrote? This may happen, even if the person does not know that there ever was such a person as Martin Luther. This is because Luther's work has influenced the tradition to which the reader has been exposed.

Suppose that you put on a pair of green sunglasses, the wrap-around kind that keeps the wearer from seeing past the edges. Then the entire world, viewed through those glasses, would have a greener tinge than would otherwise be the case. Suppose, however, that you had been born wearing such glasses, which expanded to fit you as you grew. In this scenario, there never would have been a time when you had not viewed the world through those glasses. Everything, including human skin, would appear greenish to you. This would seem obvious to you, just the way things are.

Our own presuppositions, or what we carry about with us, affect our understanding of the thoughts of others. Thus, when we read what someone else has written, we may actually be hearing that person say what we would mean if we were the ones saying it. What has happened is that the other person's ideas have been filtered through our own way of thinking, and the result may be quite different from what the other person intended to say. This especially becomes a problem when we evaluate the other person's view. Here what we may think to be an internal contradiction in that person's thought may actually be a conflict between his thought and our own. For years I have taught my students that "I don't agree" is not an adequate or even appropriate criticism of the thought of another. My master's thesis dealt with one philosopher's analysis of the thought of Plato, within which he felt he had found two contradictory concepts. My conclusion, however, was that the interpreter had actually read Plato through Aristotelian eyes, and that the conflict was not between two of Plato's ideas, but between one of Plato's and one of Aristotle's. The criticism was actually that Plato was not a very good or consistent Aristotelian, and I do not think that would have bothered Plato at all.

Having said that, we also must recognize the value of the postmodernists', and especially Derrida's, contention that every system of thought contains a contradictory element or a contradictory body of evidence, which it simply cannot assimilate. On any issue, the evidence seldom if ever is all on one side. If that were the case, controversy and disagreement would be minimal. We need to be certain that we take into account the data that contradict our own view. To ignore, suppress, or make such material fit by distorting it is an instance of the suppressing of contradictory considerations that deconstructionists decry, and to do so involves a violation of intellectual integrity.

All of this means that we must hold much of what we believe with a certain degree of tentativeness, or at least flexibility. Dogmatism on most matters is inappropriate to the actual facts of the case. We must assess the relative weight of the evidence on each side of disputed issues and place our belief and commitment on the side that appears to be supported by the greater weight of evidence. We must, however, continue to hold this commitment in tension with the contrary evidence, so that if at some point the balance of evidence shifts, we are prepared to alter our view. It also means that we must be willing to expose ourselves to contrary views, lest we suppress the truth in our zeal for our own currently held theories.

What we have said should not come as a surprise to Christians, at least to those Christians who take the Bible as their primary source of the Christian faith seriously. We have alluded earlier to the fact that the Bible never claims that we can have absolute certainty, satisfactory to human reason. Beyond that, Paul points out that our present understanding of spiritual matters is incomplete and indistinct (1 Cor. 13:12). We also believe that the phenomenon of what we sometimes call "original sin" means that we actually deceive ourselves in our understanding

(Jer. 17:9). In an earlier chapter we promised to identify points at which postmodernism is in accord with Christian belief, and these are some of those points of agreement. Note that the argument in this chapter, however, is not that postmodernism is good because it is in agreement with Christianity, but rather that it is to be considered a positive because it fits the nature of reality as we experience it, which Christianity also does.

The postmodernists, with their criticism of the Enlightenment's emphasis on the efficacy of the exclusive use of reason and experience, have pointed out that humans are not fully rational creatures. Much of human belief and action stems from more subjective factors, such as feelings. Whether such should be the case, the Enlightenment ideal of cool, dispassionate, objective attitudes is not an accurate depiction of much of human experience.

Beyond that, however, postmodernists have reminded us that there are dimensions of actual, valid knowledge that transcend the narrow scope of the scientific/mathematical method. One of these is intuition, especially as it functions in human relationships. As a seminary administrator, whose job heavily involved assessments of other human beings, I increasingly learned to trust my initial feelings about people. Sometimes, of course, these feelings had to be revised, but in many cases, subsequent experiences substantiated them.

Another large area of postmodernism's positive strength lies in the accurate emphasis, especially by Foucault, on the use of power to establish "truth." If he is correct, then the "hermeneutics of suspicion" recommended by some postmodernists is very appropriate. There is a struggle for power, a desire to get one's own way or what one wants, and in this struggle, purported knowledge is also used to accomplish one's ends. The manipulation of the truth is a real, not an imaginary, phenomenon.

One area where this is most obvious is politics. The specific title given to one of the most common forms of this practice is "spin doctoring." Spin doctors are assigned to give the most favorable interpretation possible to events that occur and to statements that their political employers make. It is interesting to see how economic events are treated. Each party is quick to take credit for positive developments, while seeking to place the blame for anything negative on the other party. If one party has recently succeeded in passing a bill that has some relationship to the matter, the opposition party blames any unfortunate development on the action, even if there has not been sufficient time for the law to have any effect. The other party, however, usually interprets such an event as an indication of just how serious is the need for such legislation, in fact, as indicating the need of even more radical action. Both sides seek to muster any considerations in support of their own views and efforts.

Such activities are especially apparent in election campaigns. Here one's own party is depicted as the very embodiment of virtue, while the opposition party is treated as the incarnation of evil and error. Data are very carefully chosen for presentation, and actions of the opposition may be severely distorted.

What is especially distressing is the basis on which the legislative process itself rests. The system of trading political favors is relied upon. I have supported your bill, so now you owe me one, and I am calling in that favor. You must vote for my bill, whether you agree with it morally or not. It is worth noting that in Lawrence Kohlberg's scale of moral development, this mutual back-scratching procedure ranks very close to the bottom.[1] And unfortunately, it is not only the official political arena that is the locus of political behavior. This can be seen in church government, educational governance, and any number of other spheres within our society.

There are numerous other ways that the truth is manipulated, or constructed. One is by the use of euphemistic descriptions. For example, Joseph Fletcher's description of the German woman who convinced a guard to impregnate her, so that she would be released from prison and could return to her family, is labeled "sacrificial adultery."[2] Al Capone, the notorious mobster of the 1920s and '30s, complained, "I have spent the best years of my life giving people the lighter pleasures, helping them have a good time, and all I get is abuse, the existence of a hunted man."[3] This is description of an action in terms of its consequences, rather than the act itself. The reverse is also true. An action may be characterized as simply "tensing the index finger of the right hand," without bothering to mention that the finger was at the time resting on the trigger of a loaded pistol, pointed at the head of a person, at point-blank range.

There may be manipulation of data. This may be done in financial reports, so that unusual items of income are included to give a better overall impression than would otherwise be the case. Other statistics also can be manipulated. Notice, for example, the widely differing estimates of the number of persons involved in a political demonstration by opposite parties in the dispute.

Subtle qualifiers enable a statement to be made that is technically true, but misleading. A joke is told of a dual track meet between the United States and the Soviet Union several years ago, won by the United States. *Pravda,* however, reported, "U.S.S.R. places second in track meet; U.S.A. finishes next to last." An actual case was the report of a denominational official to his constituency: "We have reduced the amount of interest-bearing debt." The correct translation of that statement was: "We are borrowing money from our own trust funds, and unlike the United States government, we do not pay ourselves interest."

In other cases, the manipulation of the truth is accomplished by carefully selecting the data reported, giving the impression that this sampling is representative of the whole, or is the only data. This can also be done by making sure that only one perspective is heard. In some departments of large universities, even publicly supported universities, only representatives of one school or point of view are appointed to the faculty. Unless they are unusually scrupulous in presenting alternative viewpoints, those viewpoints simply do not get heard, and even if they do, they are not presented by people who hold them with conviction. The head of the women's studies department of one university actually said, "We forbid any view that says we restrict free speech."

All in all, we conclude that there are some accurate descriptions here of the ways truth is manipulated or that power is employed to guarantee what the truth will be. It should indeed induce in us a hermeneutic of suspicion, so that we carefully evaluate the truth claims urged upon us.

Negative Criticism

For all of the helpful insights postmodernism has to offer us, there are major problems with this philosophy that deserve to be pointed out. These are of many varieties, but some of them consist in postmodernism's failure to apply its own standards and insights to itself.

One of these is the exemption of deconstruction from its own methodology. This is actually stated overtly, when Derrida says that "Justice is not deconstructible. After all, not everything is deconstructible, or there would be no point to deconstruction."[4] Why, however, should this be the case? If deconstruction is used to expose the problems of other views, why should it not be turned on itself? For if it is exempt from deconstruction, perhaps there are other ideas or ideologies that are also exempt. Unless there is some adequate justification, more than simply, "there would be no point to deconstruction," this begins to sound suspiciously like an ad hoc exception, raised in order to make one's own case. That, however, strongly resembles the sort of power knowledge to which Foucault is so emphatically opposed.

The principle of "autodeconstruction" would seem to require its application to deconstruction as well. If the presence of contradictory elements within is used against such systems of thought as Platonism, should it not also count here? Should we not be looking for the presence of contradictory elements in postmodernism and considering them as indications of defect? Certainly, the variation between what we might term "hard postmodernism" and "soft postmodernism" is a relevant consideration.

Derrida finds it very difficult to maintain his position without contradicting it in the process. We have already alluded to one of these areas in our discussion of his debate with John Searle. To speak of the idea that meaning is not supported by anything outside the text, that it is built up by the free play of words, is one thing. This is supported by Derrida's discussion of writing, the advantage of which is that it allows for differing interpretations. It is quite another thing, however, to object at great length to an interpretation of one's writing on the basis that the interpretation represents a misunderstanding and a misrepresentation. With all of Derrida's attempted avoidance of logocentrism, ontotheology, and metaphysic of presence, it is hard to understand how this objection can really be taken seriously. Derrida's response appears to be a very non-postmodern one, even on his very own terms.

To return to the limitation of deconstruction's application, we find the same problem for Derrida, but in a somewhat different setting. To insist that justice is undeconstructible gives the appearance of saying that there is something intrinsic about justice that makes it unconditionally valuable. Does this not mean that there is something of what he terms the "transcendental signified" attached to justice? Derrida maintains that this is not the case, but nonetheless wants to insist upon the undeconstructibility of justice. Just what is he saying, however? It is not at all clear, nor is any satisfactory justification given for treating justice as undeconstructible.

In other places, Derrida comes face to face with the problem and admits the difficulty. For example, having discussed the traditional or logocentric approach to meaning, he says, "We have no language—no syntax and no lexicon—which is foreign to this history; we can pronounce not a single destructive proposition which has not already had to slip into the form, the logic, and the implicit postulates of precisely what it seeks to contest."[5] This, however, seems to be a very damaging admission. To have to assume something to disprove that something is very much like the T-shirt I described earlier. In this case, its falsity entails its truth.

There are difficulties with the concept of alternative logics. It is difficult to determine just what Derrida means when he says, "It is thus not simply false to say that Mallarmé is a Platonist or a Hegelian. But it is above all not true. And vice versa."[6] At one point, he identifies his view as very close to that of Hegel, who believed that logic moved in a fashion in which there was a thesis, which then was opposed by an antithesis, and that finally these two were gathered up into a synthesis in which both were combined, elements of each surviving in the new product. Yet Derrida says that he parts company with Hegel, because there is no final synthesizing of the two. What, then, is Derrida asserting? We have seen that with respect to his own view he finally insists on rejecting an interpretation that is contrary to his, presumably on the basis that the two contradictory statements cannot both be true. It appears that he is using the idea of an alternative logic more as a rhetorical device than anything else, to break down any attempt to pin down the meaning of a statement, including his own. The selective use of such a device, however, seems somewhat evasive.

There are also problems with some of the support or arguments given for some facets of postmodernism. I have in mind here, for example, Foucault's arguments regarding power and institutions. It has been observed that this appears to be a blend of history and philosophy, as Foucault engages in analyses of how these institutions have developed historically. At times, however, he refers to what he terms "fictive" writing of history. This seems to be the sketching of things that did not necessarily happen in exactly this fashion, in order to make the point. What is the status of such fiction, however? It brings to mind a story I read in a German reader many years ago. I have no idea whether this incident ever occurred, but it is what one of my philosophy professors used to call a "metaphysical truth" — if it didn't happen, it should have. I am not introducing this as an argument for my point — this is not fictive writing of history — but as an illustration.

According to this story, Georg Hegel, the philosopher, was lecturing on the philosophy of history, showing how it illustrated the thesis-antithesis-synthesis dialectic. A student interrupted to say, "Aber, Herr Professor, die Tatsache sind ganz anders" ("But, Professor, the facts are entirely otherwise"). To this Hegel reportedly replied, "Und so schlimmer für die Tatsache" (which translates loosely as, "And so much the worse for the facts"). That seems to be what Foucault is doing and saying. The facts are being constructed to fit the theory. This is what William Dean has entitled *History Making History.*[7] This is the novel *1984*, in which history is rewritten to satisfy the point being made. It seems to be a violation of intellectual integrity, if it is really intended that someone will take this as being the actual truth. If it is not so intended, then we must ask just what function the fictive history is playing. Surely, it is something more than merely illustration, of the type sometimes referred to as "preacher stories," which are presented as if they are real — at least enough so to make plausible the point they illustrate.

It appears that Foucault is attempting to have his view prevail, or at least to obtain the results that would follow if his view were accepted, such as a more general tolerance of homosexuality. This, however, seems to be an exercise of power, of using whatever ability he has to get this view accepted as true. But is this not the very thing that he has criticized in works like *Power/Knowledge?* Here again, we find an inability to live with one's theory, or at least an unwillingness to apply the theory to itself. If, however, Foucault admits that he is doing this as an exercise of power, then are we to believe him?

This is the general problem of self-reference: the question of whether a theory can itself meet the criteria it applies to all other views. More than one theory has foundered upon this rocky shore. A generation or two ago, logical positivism had formulated a theory of meaning according to which there are only two kinds of meaningful statements. One kind is analytical in nature; that is, they make explicit in the predicate what is implicit in the subject, like mathematical statements. The other kind are those that can in theory be either verified or falsified by sensory data, like scientific statements. All other purported propositions are meaningless. Even though they may have the grammatical structure of propositions, they are actually asserting nothing. They are merely expressions of emotions.

Then, however, someone asked about the meaningfulness of this principle, which had come to be known as the verifiability criterion. What was its status? Is it an analytical statement? Certainly not. If not, then what is the set of sense data that would verify or falsify the statement that the meaning of a synthetic statement (one in which the predicate adds something not contained in the subject) is the set of sense data that would verify or falsify it? Apparently, on its own criteria, this was a meaningless statement. One attempt to respond said that it is like a ladder. Once you have climbed up on a ladder you no longer need it, and once you have used the verifiability principle, it does not matter that you see that it is meaningless. These and other attempts to salvage the principle proved unsatisfactory. The problem here as well is that if there is one area where the principle does not apply, there may likely be others as well, and the principle has been seriously breached. It appears that there is a serious problem with postmodernism, at several points.

To some extent what we are dealing with here is failure to carry a theory to the secondary level. So, for example, Rorty in effect says that truth is what works out. Does he also follow this on the next level, however? If this is a theory of what truth is, what about the truth of theories of truth? Is it the case that the theory that truth is what works out is the correct theory of truth? In other words, does holding this theory of truth work out better than holding other theories of truth? To some extent, Rorty does follow this contention, saying that pursuing those other questions (e.g., the nature of Truth) is unproductive. When he comes to measure productivity or nonproductivity, he falls back on more mirrorlike theories. In other words, the justification for holding that believing that the pragmatic test of truth is the most productive is not the productivity of this third-level belief, but the fact that it actually fits the way things are.

The postmodern objection to metanarratives falls in this category also. In various ways, the postmodernists decry metanarratives or all-inclusive philosophies. It may be simply because they cannot be constructed, or because they are constructed by the suppression of contrary voices, or simply that if adopted and practiced they have the effect of intolerance or being used oppressively. For whatever reason, whether that they cannot be done or that they must not be done, postmodernism strongly opposes metanarratives. If this is indeed the sincere view of postmodernists, then one would expect to find that they themselves would shun constructing their own metanarrative. Is this really the case, however?

I contend that postmodernism itself constitutes a metanarrative, albeit often of a somewhat different type than is customarily found. For example, the deconstruction practiced by Derrida is a universal theory. It is a claim that all theories contain contrary internal elements. It is a claim that everything, with one exception as noted above, can and must be deconstructed. It is an explanation of meaning, and how that is built up through "writing." These are encompassing explanations and theories believed to apply to all elements of reality and of human discourse. The same is true of Foucault's approach to deconstruction. His theories about power are advanced as explaining all that occurs. Power is the all-inclusive concept, applied in many different ways, but nonetheless everywhere present. It is what lies behind, not just some "knowledge," but all. This sounds strangely like a metanarrative as well.

It is clear that these theories are designed to lead to action. While decrying any sort of ontology or metaphysic of presence, these theories themselves are the basis on which practical actions are to be carried out.

One can also see, underlying the proposals, certain value systems that carry universal import. In the case of Derrida, there is a desire to overturn the totalizing of theories, which suppresses alterity. It is apparent that freedom, of a particular type, has a very high value within this system. The same is true of justice. While transcendental reference is denied, justice has an absolute character. It is what constitutes the motivation for all the deconstruction that is to be pursued. Call it what one may, the freedom-justice set of values appears strangely universal in nature. We have here what might be called a crypto-metanarratival structure.

Foucault's deconstruction is also based on certain universal elements. It is apparent that he wants to tear down any sort of coercive suppression of contrary elements. The reason for this, however, again seems to be that freedom is good and must be sought and preserved. Here is an undeconstructed element.

Note also Rorty's view of things. He states that at the age of twelve he came to the conclusion that "the point of being human was to spend one's life fighting social injustice."[8] Whether this opposition to injustice is rooted in a theory of human nature, it certainly derives from "being human," which sounds suspiciously like an implicit conception of human nature. Note that this is not phrased as if it were a view that applies to a portion of the human race, or to those in a certain culture or time period. It is a matter of "being human," so that presumably all human beings are covered by this. If this is not a metanarrative, then what is?

Although Rorty objects to what he calls Philosophy, which concerns itself with questions like what is True and what is Good, he is himself concerned with similar questions. If social injustice, cruelty, and humiliation are to be shunned, then we seem to be faced with the problem of whether these are everywhere and always wrong. Perhaps philosophy with a small *p* does not seek for the True and the Good, but when it says that the question is not "why avoid humiliating?" but rather "what humiliates?" it appears to be concerned with Humiliation or Social Injustice.[9] The question, "should we avoid humiliating?" seems to be definitely answered, "yes!" Rorty's metanarrative is what we might term the liberal-ironist (as Rorty terms his view) metanarrative, but it is a metanarrative of sorts, nevertheless.

It probably is not fair to term these full-fledged metanarratives, because they are not fully worked out, with a complete treatment of all related issues. We have used the expression "implicit metanarrative" earlier, and this is what we are dealing with here. Perhaps the way to put it is that postmodernists do not have a metanarrative, but their thought does contain a metanarrative, or it has metanarratival elements.

We should also note that the belief in the conditioning of truth is not carried through consistently. Presumably, this is true of everyone, and therefore of everyone's belief. This contention is in effect utilized to relativize or even to neutralize various viewpoints, somewhat along the lines of the genetic fallacy, that if you can explain the origin of something, you have accounted for it, and do not need to ask about its adequacy in relation to any more general criteria. This is particularly the case with Rorty's behavioristic explanation of ideas. The question to be asked, however, is whether this theory must not also be applied to postmodernism itself. Are not the contentions advanced by the postmodernists historically conditioned? So, for example, the view of freedom that seems so important to the deconstructionists is actually simply a phenomenon of our time. In particular, it draws heavily from existentialism. Does this not mean that it simply is the view of certain people in certain times and places? Why should it be treated with any greater respect than any of the other theories that have appeared? Similarly, Rorty's concern for justice (as also that of Derrida) is a product of a particular philosophy, probably utilitarianism. We may find it significant that the liberal ideals espoused by each of these men are the ideals of persons who at one time or another in their lives subscribed to some form of communism. Perhaps these are ideas that were produced by that movement and were appropriate during its time of influence, but are now outmoded, since communism is in a state of sharp decline throughout the world.

Rorty's behaviorism is especially problematic. What of those who have not had the sort of conditioning necessary to bring them to the convictions and values Rorty espouses? Can anything be said, other than, "they are different"? Do we not simply have to abandon them to the view that they hold? Or is all of the Rortian argument simply an attempt to manipulate conviction and action?

Postmodernism also generates some major practical problems. One is the concept of community as the factor introducing adequate objectivity. Right and wrong are not some absolute, universal realities, rooted in a metaphysical basis independent of humans and their judgment. Yet right and wrong are not simply individualistic, subjectivistic judgments. They are governed by the norms of the community. There is a problem here, however. How does one judge among communities, or is one's community simply that into which he or she has been born or thrust? There are alternative communities, each with its own set of standards of the right and the good. Which of these is one to follow?

More pointedly yet, what happens when communities differ and even conflict? Such conflict does occur, and on the largest and most dramatic scale, it is what we term war. If there is no measure or basis for the good and the right independent of various groups' formulations, then is not the good that which is held and practiced by the community that is able to triumph in the competition with other communities? This would seem to be a case of "might makes right," and to be a consistent application of Foucault's principles.

The problem can be seen when we consider a radical example. World War II was fought in part because of the ideology of Adolf Hitler, which included the idea of the superiority of the Aryan race and the consequent importance of ridding society of the Jews. This was an ideology strongly opposed by much of the rest of human society at the time, and certainly is widely condemned in our own time. Suppose, however, that the Axis forces had won the war. This is not as unlikely a scenario as might at first appear to be the case. If Hitler had timed the invasion of Russia a bit earlier; if the winter had not been so severe as it was; if Hitler had invaded Britain when he first planned to, rather than becoming enraged when Berlin was bombed and deciding to bomb London to the ground, thus dissipating the Luftwaffe; if Hitler had employed his jet aircraft as fighters rather than as bombers; if the weather at Dunkirk had been different at the time of the British evacuation; if all of the forces of German research in physics had been concentrated to work together — rather than inefficiently and redundantly working as independent units — so that the Germans obtained a functional atomic bomb before the United States did, the outcome of the war might have been quite different.

If all of these factors, or even several of them, had turned out differently, the Axis might well have won the war. Hitler would then have been unhampered in his efforts to carry out the extermination of the Jews, if not throughout the world, at least in a much larger geographical area and a much larger portion of the world population than he did. Would his philosophy then have been right? Would the genocide of Jews have been right? Presumably no postmodernist would be willing to answer yes to such a question, and yet that seems to be the answer that must be given on postmodern terms. For unless there is something superior to and independent of the community, then the Nazi community would be right.

There are also smaller issues of a practical and academic nature. One of these is Rorty's tactic of simply declining to discuss issues, finding them uninteresting. It is questionable whether this is an academically respectable move. It seems to be an attempt to avoid issues that would be problematic for his own view. In this respect, it resembles his statement that during his student days studying philosophy, he gradually came to the conclusion that philosophy could not construct an all-encompassing view that would tie together both Trotsky's political philosophy and the wild orchids that he studied as a boy. Only a theistic belief could do that, but he says by that time he could not see himself becoming religious, and had in fact become more raucously secular. In effect, he is saying, "It could be done, but I had lost interest." Is this an adequate answer, however? To avoid issues because they do not interest one is one thing. As soon as one advocates such an action for others, however, which Rorty does seem to be doing, a different dynamic comes into play, which seems to contradict the rationale he is advancing.

There is also a problem with the stretching of terms that often is found within postmodernism. When one denies the fixed meaning of terms, one is free to use them with any meaning one pleases, or with any meaning that emerges from the free play of words. What is unfortunate, however, is the use of words that have a rather widely accepted meaning with an intended meaning that is quite different—without notifying the reader or hearer of that unique meaning. The explanation, of course, is that the community gives the meaning. It may, however, in this case, be a very small, isolated, and unusual community that is the reference point. Forthrightness would seem to require informing the recipient of the message of what community's meaning is being used. If this is not done, then the use of such language is at best misleading.

It should be noted that at times rather unusual and dramatic terminology is used, with the rhetorical effect of seeming more impressive for being so unusual. I have in mind here Derrida's reference to "the death of the author," whereas others would utilize a more prosaic expression, like "the fallacy of authorial intent." The effect is to create the impression that something different and unusual is being said. A further problem is the practice of making two or more statements on the same issue and then alternating between them. When accused of saying "A," the postmodernist may respond, "but I said not-A in such and such a place." That may very well be true, but the person in question also said "A." This appears to be another form of evasion.

There is a difficulty with the posing of the question of how postmodernism is to be understood. The constant indications are that one has misunderstood, and indeed, must misunderstand, when attempting to understand it from an alien perspective. It is as if one can only understand postmodernism from within postmodernism. Further, there is no neutral ground into which postmodernists and non-postmodernists could enter to discuss their differences. There might be three possible answers to the question of how one can understand postmodernism:

1. From a different viewpoint, such as that of modernism.
2. From a neutral viewpoint which is neither uniquely modern nor postmodern.
3. From within postmodernism itself.

By the process of elimination, it appears that option three is the correct one. That, however, seems to call for some sort of surrender in advance. One can only understand postmodernism by becoming a postmodernist. This appears to be a tactic for eliminating any criticism, while simultaneously providing a basis for criticizing all different views. As such, however, it begs the question of the correctness of postmodernism, and is thus an illegitimate technique.

Finally, something must be said about the obscurity of style that characterizes the writing of many postmodernists. This is especially true of deconstructionists such as Derrida and Foucault, since Rorty and Fish are, by contrast, virtual models of clarity. There are many dimensions of this, and many explanations. Terms are introduced without explanation of how they are being used, and some are neologisms. References are made to conversations with other thinkers, and to other issues, without identifying them, leaving the reader to puzzle as to what is really being said. Sometimes sentences go on at great length—in one of Derrida's instances, for three pages—with various inserted quotations. One is left to wonder about such obscurity. One answer often given is that this is simply so profound that the reader does not understand; this lack of understanding, or actual misunderstanding, is made the basis of defense against charges. When, however, there is no effective effort to indicate just how the interpretation is incorrect (with the exception of Derrida's lengthy response to Searle), then one wonders if the obscurity is deliberate. In any event, it does not contribute to good communication and understanding.

There is also an unfortunate tendency in some of these postmodernists' writings to use language that is not very helpful. At times Derrida and Foucault respond to statements or ideas of others by referring to them as "ridiculous" or "stupid." Such language does not really advance the cause of learning, and in my judgment is out of place in intellectual discussions.

All of these practical problems have a deleterious effect upon scholarship and academic standards, at least as these have generally been understood. It may well be objected that this statement reveals a modern bias, an approach of objectivity, that begs the question. I propose, however, that the criteria we are appealing to are not limited to modern scholarship, but have been present through many periods of time. Such values as truthfulness, forthrightness, and offering support for contentions have, empirically, been universal values.

These are problems Allan Bloom complained about and warned of in his *Closing of the American Mind*.[10] For example, in the Vincennes branch of the University of Paris, which Foucault helped to found, grades were in some cases awarded on an unusual basis. Rather than writing a paper or taking an examination for the professor's evaluation, students could slip a piece of paper under the professor's office door, suitably inscribed with the student's self-evaluation of the learning experience in the course. This was then made the basis of the grade. In academics as with water, the result cannot rise higher than the source. Conventionally, an education has been adjudged to have value because someone of superior knowledge in the field—the professor—has judged the student to have attained a certain level of achievement, and the faculty awards the degree. The degree's value is certified by the faculty. In the type of situation just described, however, the value of the credit is certified only by the student himself or herself. It is like the man who claimed to be the smartest man in the world. When asked why one should believe that, he responded, "Because I say so." The further question was, "What weight does that statement carry?" to which the man answered, "Would the world's smartest man be wrong about something like that?"

5

BEYOND POSTMODERNISM

Where will things go from here? Some of us often wish that we could see into the future, to be able to find out where the world will go in the next hundred years or so. Yet that ability is not within human capacity. How many of us, for example, in 1988 or even early 1989, predicted what would happen politically in Eastern Europe within the year ahead? Similarly, if it were possible to predict what the stock market would do within a given twelve-month period, we could become wealthy. For that matter, if we could even predict infallibly which surfaces of a pair of dice would be turned upward at the end of the next roll of those dice, we could make a great deal of money. In this case, if we could tell what will happen to the movement known as postmodernism in the next one hundred years, it would help us to know how to prepare ourselves for the future. If we could just travel into the future, the way the crew of the *Enterprise* did in *Star Trek,* we could study what is now the future for us as history. But that only happens in science fiction.

As I sat pondering these thoughts one day, my e-mail program announced, "You have mail." All of us who have e-mail boxes have no doubt noticed the growing number and variety of messages that we receive, but this one was my most unusual ever. What particularly caught my attention was the dateline, which I assumed must be a mistake. I would like to share that e-mail with you.

Dear Professor Erickson:

Allow me to introduce myself to you. You do not know me, but I am very familiar with your work. My name is Professor Johann Bibfeldt. As an alumnus of the University of Chicago, you may be familiar with my ancestor, Franz Bibfeldt, a nineteenth-century theological scholar discovered by a group of students at Concordia Seminary, St. Louis, including a young Martin Marty. He then became something of a patron saint of the University of Chicago.

I was born in Germany in 2053 and at the time of this writing I am professor of theology at Universität Verschlossen, in Germany. I am sure you are surprised to receive this e-mail from me, because in the year 2002 humans have not yet mastered the art of time travel. We, living a hundred years later, have learned how to communicate backward in time, although we have not yet developed the ability to travel forward. I know that you are very interested in the future of evangelical theology and its relationship to postmodernism. I have made a specialty of this very subject, writing my doctoral dissertation in historical theology on the subject of evangelical theology in relationship to postmodernism in the twenty-first century. In 2102 I will present a paper entitled "Die Nachnachmoderne Evangelische Theologie im frühen Einundzwanzigten Jahrhundert" at the Deutsche

Theologische Gesellschaft. I would like to share a few of my findings with you. I will not attempt to give you my entire paper, but rather, simply to share a few brief summary remarks, which in English would be entitled "Postpostmodern Evangelical Theology in the Early Twenty-first Century."

Before commenting on early-twenty-first-century evangelical theology, I want to note briefly what had happened a century earlier. That was when the full impact of modern learning was beginning to be felt. In general, there were two major reactions by orthodox Christians. Some of them, called liberals or modernists, eagerly embraced the modern mind-set and were prepared to modify some basic Christian doctrines if necessary. On the other hand, some Christians rejected the modern learning almost completely and clung to traditional views of the Bible and their doctrines, as well as to many traditional practices. They came to be known as fundamentalists. Only later in the century were there Christians who accepted certain valid elements of the modern view and retained the content of the cardinal Christian doctrines, but modified some of the forms of expression.

I share this background to show you that by the beginning of the twenty-first century, orthodox Christians were again facing the same set of issues, this time with respect to a movement called postmodernism, that their ancestors had faced in relation to modernism a century earlier. Interestingly, the same two reactions also occurred. They demonstrated the truth of George Santayana's famous words, "Those who cannot remember the past are condemned to repeat it."[1]

One group, who came to be called postmodern evangelicals, eagerly embraced the new ideology of postmodernism.

Christianity was to be expressed in postmodern idiom. They saw their evangelical predecessors as captives of modernism who, without accepting its conclusions, had nonetheless adopted its agenda or its methodology. These evangelicals saw postmodernism as really more consonant with authentic biblical Christianity than modernism had been. Card-carrying evangelicalism had been hijacked by modernism in the twentieth century, they believed, and postmodernism constituted a sort of new reformation.

The other group reacted much as the fundamentalists had done a century earlier. They saw postmodernism as a great threat to the faith, and basically rejected everything connected with it. They continued to do theology as they had, to preach as they had. The same content of theology required the same form, as far as they were concerned.

Interestingly, the effects were much the same as in the previous century. The postmodern or progressive evangelicals increasingly became so accommodated to the culture that they were unable to speak effectively to it. They were understood, to be sure, but what they were saying increasingly became the same as what the secular culture was saying. Saddest of all, they gradually became victims of the postmodern ethic. With truth in the traditional sense deemphasized, ecclesiastical politics became the primary concern. Just as Foucault had said, power created knowledge, rather than the reverse. These evangelicals were increasingly concerned with winning political victories, with gaining positions from which they then could weave versions of the truth to sustain their positions. In a fashion reminiscent of the defense of Bill Clinton, they contended that any objections to them were simply personal attacks, yet all the while they engaged in personal attacks upon their opponents. They consistently maintained that their critics were misunderstanding and misrepresenting them, even while they themselves shifted back and forth between different positions.

The preservationists, on the other hand, lost contact with the intelligentsia. To most early-twenty-first-century intellectuals, the preservationists seemed to be a throwback to an earlier period, desperately attempting to preserve an increasingly indefensible Enlightenment mentality. They came to stress certain basic philosophical doctrines as indispensable:

1. A correspondence theory of truth
2. Foundationalism
3. A representational theory of language
4. Objectivity of thought and belief
5. An inclusive theory of reality, or a metanarrative

This list of basic beliefs came to be known as the *rudiments* of cognitive belief, and those who held them were known as rudimentalists. Some of them also displayed a rather aggressive and abrasive spirit, so that the term *rudimentalism* came to have a double meaning, referring not only to the rudiments but also to rudeness.

Now it may appear that this was largely a rerun of the twentieth century, with evangelicals making the same mistakes as they had a century earlier. Actually, there was one major difference this time. Usually conservative Christians have been reactive rather than proactive. They often are the last ones really to grasp what is happening culturally and intellectually, and they then adopt a view about the time those in the broader culture or broader theology are abandoning it. So they proceed to state the ideas and arguments which sound new and fresh to evangelicals, but which are actually retreads of liberal ideas of a generation earlier.

In this case, there was a third group, which saw a certain amount of validity in postmodernism. For example, they recognized the truth of the conditioning effect upon the thought of everyone located in a particular time and place culturally. They also recognized the limitations of the scientific method. They saw that in certain areas, such as personal knowledge, other factors than simply intellectual cogitation are involved, including intuition. They saw that truth frequently is better communicated in narrative than in propositional form. And they recognized the value of a community as a check upon the unbalanced understanding that we can fall into if we function in isolation.

My description may have led you to believe that they were actually postmodern evangelicals. They did not, however, simply absorb postmodernism uncritically. They saw its problems. They observed that for all of their disclaimers, the postmodernists were unable to escape certain perennial characteristics of truth and of communication. And so, rather than accepting postmodernism without modifications, or retreating to a pre-postmodernism, they became postpostmodernists. They insisted that while drawing on the valid insights of postmodernism, it is essential to go beyond it at a number of crucial points.

What the postpostmodern evangelicals were doing was not just seeking to formulate a postmodern or a postpostmodern view, but rather, to arrive at a perennialist conception of truth. They contended that there are certain elements involved or presupposed in every effort to articulate one's view, and especially when the assumption is made that the other person can understand what is being said and hopefully be persuaded of this view.

Quite a number of factors led these postpostmodern evangelicals to conclude that postmodernism must be transcended. For one thing, they saw signs of the next movement beginning to appear, even at the turn of the century. You know that at any given time you can find representatives of several different ideologies coexisting simultaneously. In the late twentieth century, there were postmodernists, modernists, and even premodernists simultaneously, even within American society. While one philosophy is in severe decline and even virtual eclipse, another is in ascendancy and yet another is beginning to rise. So those who were wise and alert were on the watch for the first glimmers of postpostmodernism. While some postmodernists seemed to think that the final period and the final ideology had been reached, these scholars recognized that postmodernism was also a historical phenomenon, conditioned by its situation in time and culture. They knew that every ideology up until that time had eventually been displaced, and that this one would be also. They reasoned that because social and intellectual change was taking place much more rapidly in the late twentieth century than it had previously, postmodernism would have a shorter life span than modernism had. Further, because of certain contradictory elements within postmodernism, they reasoned that it was inherently unstable and would therefore fade more rapidly.

The signs that they read were available for anyone to see.

They saw that Derrida, for example, while claiming that every ideology autodeconstructs because it contains its own contradictory within it,[2] maintained that deconstruction itself could not be deconstructed, and that while everything else must be deconstructed in the light of justice, justice itself could not be deconstructed.[3] They saw that this very claim to exemption constituted an internal contradiction to the theory, and thus entailed deconstruction's own autodeconstruction. They saw that Foucault, while contending that power created truth, was unwilling to admit that he himself was attempting to establish his own view by the use of power. In a sense, these postpostmodernists were better postmodernists than were the postmodernists themselves, for they extended the idea of historical conditioning to every theory, including postmodernism and postpostmodernism. Where they differed was in attempting to find ways of neutralizing or reducing this conditioning.

They saw signs that postmodernism was beginning to suffer defections. They read, for example, the statement by Barbara Johnson, Derrida's translator, "It is not possible to show that the belief in truth is an error without implicitly believing in the notion of Truth. By the same token, to show that the binary oppositions of metaphysics are illusions is *also*, and perhaps most importantly, to show that such illusions cannot simply in turn *be opposed* without repeating the same illusion."[4] They knew that sooner or later postmodernists like Johnson would not be able to live with the tension, even if Derrida could. They saw the opposite reactions of postmodernists to Derrida's ninety-two-page response[5] to John Searle's eleven-page critique of his thought,[6] and knew that the synthesis was fragile.[7] They knew that once the fictive writing of history was adopted, conflicting views would eventually lead to the disintegration of postmodernism. They read the words of a late-twentieth-century literature professor named Bloom: "Either there were aesthetic values, or there are only the overdeterminations of race, class, and gender. You must choose, for if you believe that all value ascribed to poems or plays or novels and stories is only a mystification in the service of the ruling class, then why should you read at all rather than go forth to serve the desperate needs of the exploited classes?" While you may identify that quotation as being from Allan Bloom, in *The Closing of the American Mind*,[8] it is actually from Harold Bloom, a onetime deconstructionist, in *The Western Canon*.[9]

The postpostmodern evangelicals also saw signs of a shift toward a more conservative view of values. They noted the change toward more conservative attitudes in sexual morality, the increasing percentage of virginity among teenagers, and the decline of the stigma attached to it. The public reaction, not only to the White House capers of William Jefferson Clinton, but to the postmodern type of defense of his actions, and the sense that tragedies like Columbine High School and Wedgwood Baptist Church were not simply pragmatically problematic but contrary to the very nature of things, encouraged them. They saw in one issue of *U.S. News and World Report* two articles that indicated a shift. One described the action of the Central Council of Rabbis of Reformed Judaism, encouraging a return to traditional practices.[10] The other described the move in art, where even some former conceptualists were returning to more traditional criteria of beauty, representation, and craftsmanship.[11] The postpostmodernists observed with interest the reactions, even by Stanley Fish, to *Dutch,* Edmund Morris's biography of Ronald Reagan. Some popular musicians, such as Billy Joel and Paul McCartney, began to compose classical music.

They also noted the "retro" phenomena. For example, in 1997, the Volkswagen car company introduced a model called the New Beetle. Beneath the surface, this was a thoroughly modern automobile, utilizing the same chassis and drive train as the Volkswagen Golf. The external appearance, however, was quite different. The car bore a striking resemblance to the Old Beetle, which Volkswagen had manufactured, with gradual changes, from the 1930s through the '70s. Although there were notable differences between the body of the New Beetle and the Old Beetle, the resemblance was strong enough to justify retaining the name "Beetle." Volkswagen priced the car quite inexpensively. To their amazement, however, the demand for the car was extremely strong, and the list price was soon raised. In 2000, the Chrysler Corporation (later the Chrysler division of DaimlerChrysler) brought out a retro car of their own, the Chrysler PT Cruiser. As with the New Beetle, beneath the body was a modern mechanical system, based upon the Plymouth/Dodge Neon. The body of the car, however, resembled something from the 1930s. Demand for the vehicle was so strong that dealers were soon asking (and receiving) $10,000 over list price.

The cultural changes were even becoming apparent in such a realm as sports. One of the first indications was the decision of the major league baseball offices in 2001 that umpires should begin calling what was known as "the high strike." The rule book was quite clear that a pitch that crossed home plate between the batter's knees and a point midway between the shoulder and the belt was a strike. For years, however, the umpires had simply ignored that rule. Any pitch above the waist was called a ball. Now, however, umpires were instructed to follow the rule book in their calling of strikes. While pitchers rejoiced and batters mourned this change of policy, another development had the opposite effect, namely, the elimination of the "outside strike." Again the rule book was quite explicit that a pitch must pass over the plate in order to be called a strike. Some pitchers, however, began a game by throwing the ball just off the outside corner of the plate, and if they found that the umpire consistently called such a pitch a strike, continued to move farther and farther outside. The result was that batters had to lean out over the plate in order to reach such "strikes," whereupon the pitcher would throw a legal strike on the inside corner of the plate, moving the batter back. When, however, umpires were instructed that they were to follow the rule book regarding the horizontal limits of the strike zone, pitchers complained and batters celebrated. These returns to objective standards in administration of the rules were another indication of a cultural swing.

Still other indications were emerging. To the surprise of many, sales of business suits began to increase as a movement away from casual dress began. The stock market decline of 2000–2001, especially of technology stocks, took many by surprise and indicated that Alan Greenspan was right about "irrational exuberance." While it may seem strange that the decline of popularity of tech stocks indicated a move toward a more rational approach to investing, it was the case. For although technology is one of the most rational areas of our culture, the enthusiasm for tech stocks was not based upon a rational analysis of value, since some of these, especially the internet stocks, had no earnings and no immediate prospect of earnings. Those who had bid up the price of these stocks did so, not from rational but from emotional influences, and the decline in stock prices of 90 percent and more introduced the reality of rational factors. Many had touted the "new economy," even ridiculing those who failed to see that a paradigm shift had taken place. The severe effects of the market decline on the new economy were a further indication of a return toward earlier values.

On September 11, 2001, a terrorist attack against the United States led to the destruction of the World Trade Center in New York City and damage to the Pentagon. Some immediate effects, such as an increase in church attendance, soon declined, and there were even some indications of an increased belief in moral relativity. There were more subtle but longer-termed sobering effects, however. Concern about family increased, as did sales of Bibles and religious symbols.

It also became increasingly apparent, first to the postpostmodern evangelicals and then to broader society, that postmodernism could not survive, from practical considerations. This first began to occur at the level of some of the most prestigious universities. When students began to ask, "Why should I enroll here, to be indoctrinated in the belief that I am the locus and criterion of truth?" their parents also began to question why they should pay in excess of $20,000 per year to enable their children to learn that they did not need to learn. Enrollment began to drop off rapidly, as did financial support. "Seinfeld universities" — universities about nothing — appeared to soon be truly universities of no one. Almost in a panic, university administrators and even faculty began to react.

This also carried over to Christian institutions. Some megachurches that had built their appeal on a basically postmodern type of ministry did not simply decline, they crashed. Because their constituents did not have long-term or emphatic commitment to the church and had not been discipled much beyond their initial commitments, they quickly abandoned the church when something more attractive came along. In some cases, these local congregations lost their church property to the lender through foreclosure.

There was also a shift in television viewing. With the increased popularity of cable television, viewership of the major broadcast channels declined. Cable programming included more cultural material in many cases, and even made available, through nostalgia channels like Nick at Nite and TV Land, programs conveying the values of an earlier period. Even some network programming began to change, in part as a result of the activities of organizations such as the Parents Television Council. Among the one-hour programs, like *Judging Amy, Family Law,* and *Providence,* more traditional values were proving viable. Similarly the good reception given to the movie *Lord of the Rings* indicated a resumption of interest in more objective values.

Even advertisements indicated that the culture was changing. In one ad for a popular painkiller, a woman told of her headache problems, then said, "Medications don't remove pain; information does." She then cited scientific studies indicating the efficacy of this particular over-the-counter pain medication. Her comment was, "Information really is power, at least where pain is concerned." This was one of the first indications that those who do research on human behavior as it affects sales appeal were finding it profitable to appeal to rational, factual thinking.

The moral and intellectual emptiness of postmodernism was becoming apparent to more and more intellectuals. The conversion of political figures such as Charles Colson, media personalities like Jane Fonda, and athletes like Daryl Strawberry and Deion Sanders, and the movement to theological orthodoxy of theologians like Thomas Oden, a self-described onetime "movement theologian," were signs of a beginning trend.

It was not, however, just a matter of being unable to generate an adequate ethic, particularly a social ethic, that pointed up a serious lack in postmodernism. The problem went further than that. To some, it appeared that postmodernism actually undercut the possibility of making serious ethical judgments. For example, feminists observed that after a long period in which women had been deprived of equal rights with men, they were just beginning to come into their own in the pursuit of justice and equality. At this very time, however, postmodernism in effect denied the possibility of making any sorts of moral judgments that transcended one's own opinion and vested interest. This appeared to feminists to be a case of those with power changing the rules in such a way as to maintain their own situation. Racial minorities began to complain as well, saying that just when their complaints that they were being discriminated against were being heard, postmodernism removed the very basis for making such judgments. So these postpostmodern evangelicals, who did believe in an objective basis for judgments of right and wrong, found themselves with somewhat unexpected allies, including some who were not especially religious.

Even in politics signs of change were appearing. The Jesse Ventura/John McCain phenomenon indicated that voters, especially younger voters, were tired of politics as usual and desired some clear, unequivocal, and honest answers to questions. They were tired of being massaged and manipulated.

Some more perceptive members of society began to see that the repercussions from postmodernism were starting to threaten the very foundations of society itself. With the evaporation of belief in the traditional basis for ethical values, postmodern grounds, such as Rorty's irony, were supposed to replace them. This, however, was not working. Fear that intellectual anarchy would lead to political anarchy led increasing numbers of people to a concern for more substantial ethical and behavioral standards.

In addition, those who were to become the postpostmodern evangelicals observed the shifting balance of power and influence from Europe and North America to Third World people. This was perhaps apparent to the evangelicals sooner than for others because their contact with the Third World churches led them to see that the momentum and the growth in the church was clearly there. Although some characteristics of Third World life and society were hospitable to postmodernism, such as the less rationalistic worldviews, there were some points on which the Third World was actually quite hostile to postmodernism. Good and evil were very real matters for persons from Africa, for example. Similarly, as Christians from countries formerly behind what Winston Churchill had labeled "the Iron Curtain" began to assert themselves in ecclesiastical and theological discussions, they brought a conservative emphasis with them. They had seen the reality of evil in communism, and wanted no part of relativism. It began to appear that high postmodernism was restricted to more highly developed countries, and especially to the leisure classes that had the luxury of indulging themselves in this sort of thinking. For the average person, struggling to survive economically and in other ways in this world, postmodern philosophies appeared to display a rather unreal quality.

These changes presented an unusual opportunity for an ideology that returned to objectivity and truth. Several steps were involved in these scholars formulating a postpostmodern evangelical theology. They did some important philosophical, and especially epistemological, work:

1. They disdained the superficial dismissal of foundationalism, which usually treats all foundationalism as that of Descartes or Locke, and developed a much more sophisticated "neofoundationalism." Some of the early models for this came from the work of Robert Audi and William Alston. This type of foundationalism did not claim the sort of absolute certainty that Descartes thought he had attained, but simply observed that one has to start somewhere.

2. They saw that all attempts to communicate one's view and to advocate it against others assumes a sort of primitive or prereflective correspondence view of truth, on a more basic level than correspondence, coherence, or pragmatic tests of truth.

3. They argued for the inevitability of some sort of holoscopic conception, contending that even postmodernism has its metanarratival elements. They particularly noted Rorty's observation

that there was one way to develop a metanarrative, namely, on the basis of a theism, and carried through on that suggestion.

4. They developed new types of apologetics, beginning with elements within the experience of postmoderns, but went on to offer arguments that the insufficiency of postmodern thought and life seemed to cry out for.

5. They utilized the communication power of narrative, both in their theology and in their preaching. They worked hard at finding ways of communication that dealt with the sound bite, video game, MTV mentality. This involved the use of narrative and dramatic methods. To reach beyond the purely cerebral, they developed their imagination and creativity by reading such comic strips and cartoons as "The Far Side," "Close to Home," "Strange Brew," the sports-oriented "In the Stands," and the business-oriented "Bottom Liners." They themselves found different ways to communicate the Christian message, such as through the comic strip "B. C.," the television ads for the *Power for Living* book, the *Jesus* video, and the "God" billboards. Even professors employed such techniques as drama, role play, dialogical lectures, case studies, and the Socratic method in their teaching.

6. They utilized communities of discussion, not as establishing the objectivity of truth, but as reducing subjectivity. While not denying the subjective and conditioned nature of each person's beliefs, they found ways to reduce that subjectivity and its effects, or to increase intersubjectivity. One major endeavor related to the problem of historical conditioning. The postpostmodernist evangelicals recognized and conceded the effect of such conditioning. They realized, however, that if they were to discuss these views with others and to argue for one view over against another, they

could not simply accept this fact of the conditioning effect. They strove to find ways to reduce the effect of conditioning upon their thinking. This involved a number of factors.

One of these was to examine their own backgrounds, to attempt to identify the factors that had borne upon them and influenced their understanding and belief. This was the writing of their own intellectual autobiographies. Into this went a number of considerations: their nationality, their geographical community, the views of the parents, their gender, the kinds of teachings to which they were exposed in their most formative years. They were then able to make compensations for these factors, to try to neutralize, to some extent, the influences that had shaped them.

They also exposed themselves to differing viewpoints than their own. This included cross-cultural conversations with persons from other segments of their own society, and from other parts of the world. It also meant interacting with persons of other intellectual traditions, even within their own society. It entailed grappling with the views of ages other than their own. In many cases, this meant reading the thoughts of these others.

I suggested earlier that this postpostmodernism was a case of evangelicals being in the vanguard, rather than the rear, of developments. Given their concern, they sought for ways to hasten the transition to this next stage. They employed several techniques:

1. They developed an "ideological simulator," to enable people to experience the consequences of postmodernism. "Simulators" had been present in a number of fields for some time. Flight simulators were used extensively in training airline

pilots, and driving simulators were used to train and test professional drivers. Human body simulators were used to train physicians, especially surgeons. At the Olympic Village in Lillehammer, Norway, where the 1994 Winter Olympics had been held, there was a bobsled simulator, which enabled persons to experience the thrill of a bobsled ride. The postpostmodern evangelicals found ways to devise ideological simulators. Taking a cue from a financial counseling firm that had an on-line "fright simulator," enabling people to experience what a severe bear market would be like, they found ways to simulate the consequences of postmodernism. These involved, among other things, case studies, such as that at the Vincennes campus of the University of Paris, which Foucault helped to found, where students received credit, not by attending class and submitting papers, but by slipping a note under the professor's door, giving their own self-assigned grades.

2. They began to compile first-person stories of postmodernaholics, especially of college students. For example, one young woman, studying at a notable postmodern university, was asked on an examination to define the word *juxtapose*. Not knowing the meaning of the word, she wrote, in jest, "'Juxtapose' means 'cat.' Since Heidegger said that reality is as we perceive it, this is what 'juxtapose' means to me." To her surprise, she received a perfect score for her answer, and the professor praised her for insight. It was the beginning of her disillusionment with postmodernism and her eventual conversion to faith in Christ. Asking herself, "Why should I pay tuition to learn that I create my own truth?" she sought for a truth that was more than simply human opin-

ion. Postmoderns Anonymous was founded, complete with a twelve-step recovery program, and soon grew rapidly.

3. While these methods were helpful with cases of chronic postmodernism, the postpostmodernists saw that acute post-modernism required more powerful intervention. Specially trained counselors were able to administer intellectual shock therapy. Recognizing that postmodernism is not only an intellectual but also an existential condition, a group of therapists of the Kierkegaardian school developed. They found ways to push postmodernists to despair, and in acute cases, help those who were already at the point of making the leap, to transition to Christian faith.

4. They observed that many postmodernists, while advocating narrative, often did so through the use of propositional arguments and logistic lectures. They pointed out that such persons were actually primary postmodernists, but secondary and tertiary modernists. They themselves began to create truly narrative ways to do theology under controlled interpretive conditions, thus exposing the insincerity and inconsistency of claimed postmodernists.

5. They worked hard at bringing postmoderns to see the incompatibility of some ideas that they had eclectically combined. In the case of those with some Christian inclinations, for example, they helped them see the fundamental antithesis between Christ's way and view of life and the ways of the world. So, for example, persons who claimed to be born-again Christians but also believed in reincarnation were helped to see that they were neither genuinely Christian nor New Age, but had to choose between the two.

6. They found ways to starve off postmodernism from resources to which it had no legitimate claim. They did this by continually reminding postmoderns of their own views, and insisting that they apply to their own ideologies those criteria that they imposed upon others. For example, they insisted that criticism of metanarratives must be applied to the crypto-metanarratives employed by postmodernists. Postmodernism was living on borrowed capital, and the postpostmodernists helped to call in the loan.

7. They worked hard at breaking down the distinction between the theoretical and the practical, while pointing out inconsistencies between the postmodernists' theory and their practice. In theological seminaries, for example, they set up truly postmodern models of ministry, and students were quickly able to see, when their fellow students exercised such models upon them, the unworkability of such models of ministry and even of the Christian life. In short, they showed that postmodernism failed the tests, both of classical pragmatism and of neopragmatism.

8. They insisted upon being genuinely and validly global. They personally did this by involving themselves in study groups made up of persons from around the world. In some cases, they were able to accomplish this end through interaction with international students and immigrants, in which they did more listening than talking, and genuinely listened to what the internationals were truly saying. They observed that what claimed to be postmodernism was actually frequently quite Euro-American, and male, Anglo, and middle class as well. As such, it was actually crypto-modern. The postpostmodernists sought the insight of a world community.

After hearing what I have written, you might simply assume that by 2102, postpostmodernism will have become the dominant view. The truth of the matter is that postpostmodernism was soon supplanted, first by postpostpostmodernism and then postpostpostpostmodernism. I believe that now, in 2102, I already see the beginnings of postpostpostpostpostmodernism appearing. But of course, treating that would require more space than we have here.

There is perhaps one question that you have after hearing about this, namely, was Millard J. Erickson one of those who led the move to postpostmodernism? No, I am afraid that by the beginning of the period we are discussing, he had retired. The prime movers in that development were the younger evangelical scholars, some of them former students of Erickson, whose names may not be household words to you in 2002, but some of whom may actually be in college, seminary, or graduate school in your day, or be reading books like *The Postmodern World*.

Thank you very much for allowing me to share these insights. I hope they are of some interest and some help to you and to anyone else with whom you may choose to share them.

Sincerely,
Doktor Johann Bibfeldt
Professor der Systematische Theologie
Universität Verschlossen

And now that we know the direction of the future, you and I can be part of bringing it to pass.

NOTES

Chapter 2: Postmodernism in the University

1 Francis A. Schaeffer, *The God Who Is There: Speaking Historic Christianity into the Twentieth Century* (Chicago: InterVarsity, 1968), pp. 15-16.

2 Jacques Derrida, *Writing and Difference* (Chicago: University of Chicago Press, 1978), pp. 279-80.

3 Ibid., p. 280.

4 Michel Foucault, "Truth and Power," in *Power/Knowledge,* ed. Colin Gordon (New York: Pantheon, 1980), p. 133.

5 Richard Rorty, "Introduction: Pragmatism and Philosophy," in *Consequences of Pragmatism* (Minneapolis: University of Minnesota Press, 1982), pp. 14-16.

6 Richard Rorty, *Contingency, Irony, and Solidarity* (Cambridge: Cambridge University Press, 1989), p. 17.

7 Jacques Derrida, *On the Name,* ed. Thomas Dutoit (Stanford, Calif.: Stanford University Press, 1995), p. 120.

8 Derrida, *Writing and Difference,* p. 285.

9 Richard Rorty, "Trotsky and the Wild Orchids," in *Wild Orchids and Trotsky: Messages from American Universities,* ed. Mark Edmundson (New York: Penguin, 1993), pp. 41-42.

10 Rorty, "Private Irony and Liberal Hope," in *Contingency, Irony, and Solidarity,* p. 85.

11 Stanley Fish, *Is There a Text in This Class? The Authority of Interpretive Communities* (Cambridge, Mass.: Harvard University Press, 1980), p. 305.

12 Ibid., p. 306.

13 Ibid., p. 310.

14 Richard Rorty, "Solidarity or Objectivity?" in *Objectivity, Relativism, and Truth* (Cambridge: Cambridge University Press, 1991), pp. 22-23.

15 Jacques Derrida, *Dissemination,* translated with an introduction and additional notes by Barbara Johnson (Chicago: University of Chicago Press, 1981), p. 207.

Chapter 3: Postmodernism and Christianity

1 George Barna, *The Barna Report: What Americans Believe* (Ventura, Calif.: Regal, 1991), pp. 84-85.

2 George Barna, *The Barna Report 1992–93: America Renews Its Search for God* (Ventura, Calif.: Regal, 1992), pp. 76-78, 294-95.

3   J. Gresham Machen, *Christianity and Liberalism* (Grand Rapids, Mich.: Eerdmans, 1923), pp. 7-8.

4   Jacques Derrida, "Limited Inc. a b c . . . ," in *Glyph 2*, ed. Samuel Weber and Henry Sussman (Baltimore: Johns Hopkins University Press, 1977), pp. 162-253.

5   Dallas Willard, address to the Evangelical Theological Society, Santa Clara, Calif., November 21, 1997.

Chapter 4: Postmodernism: Good, Bad, or Indifferent?

1   Lawrence Kohlberg, *The Philosophy of Moral Development: Moral Stages and the Idea of Justice* (San Francisco: Harper & Row, 1981).

2   Joseph Fletcher, *Situation Ethics: The New Morality* (Philadelphia: Westminster, 1966), pp. 164-165.

3   Quoted in Dale Carnegie, *How to Win Friends and Influence People* (New York: Simon and Schuster, 1948), p. 21.

4   Jacques Derrida, *Deconstruction in a Nutshell: A Conversation with Jacques Derrida,* edited with a commentary by John D. Caputo (New York: Fordham University Press, 1997), pp. 131-32.

5   Jacques Derrida, *Writing and Difference* (Chicago: University of Chicago Press, 1978), pp. 280-81.

6   Jacques Derrida, *Dissemination,* translated with an introduction and additional notes by Barbara Johnson (Chicago: University of Chicago Press, 1981), p. 207.

7   William D. Dean, *History Making History: The New Historicism in American Religious Thought* (Albany: State University of New York Press, 1988).

8   Richard Rorty, "Trotsky and the Wild Orchids," in *Wild Orchids and Trotsky: Messages from American Universities,* ed. Mark Edmundson (New York: Penguin, 1993), p. 35.

9   Rorty, "Private Irony and Liberal Hope," in *Contingency, Irony, and Solidarity* (Cambridge: Cambridge University Press, 1989), p. 91.

10   David Allan Bloom, *The Closing of the American Mind: How Higher Education Has Failed Democracy and Impoverished the Souls of Today's Students* (New York: Simon and Schuster, 1987).

Chapter 5: Beyond Postmodernism

1   George Santayana, *The Life of Reason or the Phases of Human Progress,* 2nd ed. (New York: Charles Scribner's Sons, 1936), vol. I, p. 284; one-vol. rev. ed. (New York: Charles Scribner's Sons, 1953), p. 82. (The notes for this chapter are from Bibfeldt's e-mail.)

2   Jacques Derrida, *Deconstruction in a Nutshell: A Conversation with Jacques*

Derrida, edited with a commentary by John D. Caputo (New York: Fordham University Press, 1997), p. 9.

3   Ibid., pp. 131-32.

4   Barbara Johnson, translator's introduction to Derrida, *Dissemination,* translated with an introduction and additional notes by Barbara Johnson (Chicago: University of Chicago Press, 1981), p. x.

5   Jacques Derrida, "Limited Inc. a b c . . . ," in *Glyph 2,* ed. Samuel Weber and Henry Sussman (Baltimore: Johns Hopkins University Press, 1977), pp. 162-253.

6   John R. Searle, "Reiterating the Differences: A Reply to Derrida," in *Glyph 1,* ed. Samuel Weber and Henry Sussman (Baltimore: Johns Hopkins University Press, 1977), pp. 198-208.

7   John M. Ellis, *Against Deconstruction* (Princeton, N.J.: Princeton University Press, 1989), pp. 13-14, n. 10.

8   David Allan Bloom, *The Closing of the American Mind: How Higher Education Has Failed Democracy and Impoverished the Souls of Today's Students* (New York: Simon and Schuster, 1987).

9   Harold Bloom, *The Western Canon: The Books and Schools of the Ages* (New York: Harcourt Brace, 1994), p. 522.

10   Jeffery L. Sheler, "The Reformed Reform," *U.S. News and World Report,* June 7, 1999, p. 56.

11   Jay Tolson, "What's After Modern?" *U.S. News and World Report,* June 7, 1999, pp. 50-52

GENERAL INDEX

SCRIPTURE INDEX